D0190887

Budgeting for
Non-Financial
Managers

SMARTER SOLUTIONS

The finance pack

Budgeting for Non-Financial Managers

How to master and maintain effective budgets

IAIN MAITLAND

Prentice Hall

London • New York • Toronto • Sydney • Tokyo • Singapore •
Madrid • Mexico City • Munich • Paris

PEARSON EDUCATION LIMITED

Head Office:
Edinburgh Gate
Harlow CM20 2JE
Tel: +44 (0)1279 623623
Fax: +44 (0)1279 431059

London Office:
128 Long Acre
London WC2E 9AN
Tel: +44 (0)207 447 2000
Fax: +44 (0)207 240 5771
www.business-minds.com

First published in Great Britain in 1996

© Pearson Education Limited 2000

The right of Iain Maitland to be identified as author of this work has been asserted by him in accordance with the Copyright, Designs, and Patents Act 1988.

ISBN 0 273 64494 7

British Library Cataloguing in Publication Data
A CIP catalogue record for this book can be obtained from the British Library.

10 9 8 7 6 5 4 3

Typeset by Northern Phototypesetting Co. Ltd, Bolton
Printed and bound in Great Britain by Biddles Ltd, Guildford and King's Lynn

The Publishers' policy is to use paper manufactured from sustainable forests.

Contents

So you want to master budgeting?

Budgeting for Non-Financial Managers is written for you – the manager with little or no financial knowledge or experience who is responsible for planning and/or keeping to a sales, production, capital expenditure or departmental budget, such as marketing or administration. On a clear, step-by-step basis, this book takes you through each and every stage of the process, telling you all you need to know about it.

Chapter 1, 'What you need to know about budgeting' introduces you to the subject – in particular, the different types of budget drawn up, the advantages and disadvantages of budgeting and the budgetary procedures that are followed in most firms. Chapter 2, 'How to prepare budget forecasts' then shows you how to compile key, preparatory notes for your departmental budget forecast or whatever, by gathering information, anticipating revenues and estimating expenditure over the coming period.

> On a clear, step-by-step basis, this book takes you through each and every stage of the process, telling you all you need to know about it.

Chapter 3, 'How to compose budget forecasts' explains what to do with these invaluable notes, by creating a form, accumulating the contents and producing the final version of your budget forecast. Chapter 4, 'What you need to know about submitting budget forecasts' sets out the role of a budget committee, how to participate successfully in budget meetings and explains how a master budget is developed for the whole organisation.

Chapter 5, 'How to keep track of budgets' indicates the importance of establishing suitable monitoring procedures for your situation, and works through the numerous ways of studying revenues and checking expenditure so that your budget form is completed properly. Chapter 6, 'How to adhere to budgets' discusses how to identify

To illustrate and enhance the text, the book also contains a wide and diverse range of model budget forecasts, forms and budgets, various types of checklist and case studies.

significant variances, achieve revenues, control expenditure and make changes to this budget, others and the master budget, when necessary.

Chapter 7, 'Budgeting: common questions and answers' raises all of the questions you might have about forecasting budgets, setting the master budget and managing budgets – and answers them for you. Chapter 8, 'Budgeting: typical problems and solutions' investigates the problems that occur with regard to the profit budget, cash budget and projected annual accounts that form the master budget, and goes through possible solutions.

To illustrate and enhance the text, the book also contains a wide and diverse range of model budget forecasts, forms and budgets, various types of checklist and case studies which should help to increase your knowledge and understanding of the different stages of the budgeting process. Complete with chapter summaries, a conclusion which reviews the key points of the entire book, and an extensive glossary of terms, *Budgeting for Non-Financial Managers* makes essential reading before, during and after your budget has been set.

Iain Maitland

Budgeting is the process of compiling budgets and subsequently adhering to them as closely as possible.

CHAPTER ONE

What you need to know about budgeting

- Types of budget

- The advantages of budgeting

- The disadvantages of budgeting

- Budgetary procedures

- Summary

So what exactly is 'budgeting'? It may be defined quite simply as 'the process of compiling budgets and subsequently adhering to them as closely as possible'. To begin with, it is sensible to take an introductory look at this whole process, putting it into its overall context within a firm. To do this properly, you need to consider the different types of budget that are composed, the advantages and disadvantages of budgeting *and* the budgetary procedures which are followed by many organisations.

Types of budget

A 'budget' can best be described as a 'financial plan that sets out anticipated revenues and/or estimated expenditures over a forthcoming period of time, typically one year'. Invariably, numerous budgets will be drawn up within a business. The most common ones are as follows:

- sales budget
- production budget
- capital expenditure budget
- departmental budgets
- master budget.

Sales budget

As indicated by its name, this budget details the total sales expected over a given period such as a year, and is sub-divided into shorter periods, usually of one month's duration each.

Sales will be shown in terms of their quantities and/or values and are often viewed by product groups, sales agents' territories or markets, as appropriate. An extract from a basic sales budget can be seen as Figure 1.1.

Notes to examples
(1) Unless otherwise stated, all the examples given are separate, and independent of each other.
(2) All examples are fictionalised, and included to show the basic principles of budgeting.
(3) Some examples are incorporated to illustrate the varied approach to budget forms, contents and activities taken within different forms. These examples tend to be simplified so that the underlying principles are not obscured.

SALES BUDGET 2000		January			February			March		
		Est.	Act.	Var.	Est.	Act.	Var.	Est.	Act.	Var.
Wayliner Mark I	Volume	500			550			700		
	Price	50			50			50		
	Value	25,000			27,500			35,000		
Wayliner Mark II	Volume	500			550			850		
	Price	50			50			50		
	Value	25,000			27,500			42,500		
Wayliner Mark II	Volume	550			650			700		
	Price	60			60			60		
	Value	33,000			39,000			42,000		
Wayliner Duo	Volume	450			550			600		
	Price	80			80			80		
	Value	36,000			44,000			48,000		
Total Values		119,000			138,000			167,500		

Wayliner Mark I etc.: Categories by product group, sales representative's territory or market typically volume/price/value: in units, £ sterling and £ sterling respectively.

Est/Act/Var: 'Estimated', 'actual' and 'variance'. All three columns need to be included to ensure the budget is monitored carefully.

The complete budget would have a 'Totals' column to the far right after 'December'.

Please note that Figures 1.1 to 1.10 are independent and unrelated to each other.

Figure 1.1   Sales budget: an extract

Production budget

The production budget specifies the various quantities of goods to be produced throughout the period in question, as well as the costs of the direct materials, direct labour and factory overheads involved in producing these amounts.

'Direct materials' are those raw items and component parts which are incorporated into the finished goods. 'Direct labour' refers to that part of the workforce which actually produces the goods. 'Factory overheads' are those other production expenses like indirect materials, indirect labour and heat, light and power. See Figure 1.2 as an example of a simplified production budget.

PRODUCTION BUDGET 2000		January			February			March		
		Est.	Act.	Var.	Est.	Act.	Var.	Est.	Act.	Var.
Opening stock level		8,000			10,000			12,000		
Sales volume		4,000			5,000			6,000		
Closing stock requirement		10,000			12,000			14,000		
Production requirement		6,000			7,000			8,000		
Materials:										
MKP 127	Volume	6,000			7,000			8,000		
	Price	5.25			5.25			5.00		
	Value	31,500			36,750			40,000		
TLM 367	Volume	18,000			21,000			24,000		
	Price	3.75			3.50			3.50		
	Value	67,500			73,500			84,000		
Total materials (£)		99,000			110,250			124,000		
Labour:										
Skilled	Volume	3,000			3,500			4,000		
	Price	12.75			12.75			12.75		
	Value	38,250			44,625			51,000		
Semi-skilled	Volume	3,000			3,500			4,000		
	Price	8.25			8.25			8.25		
	Value	24,750			28,875			33,000		
Total labour (£)		63,000			73,500			84,000		
Overheads:										
Depreciation		10,000			10,000			10,000		
Repairs, maintenance		3,000			3,000			3,000		
Heat, light, power		1,500			1,500			1,500		
Indirect wages		7,000			7,000			7,000		
Total overheads (£)		21,500			21,500			21,500		
Grand total (£)		183,500			205,250			229,500		

Opening stock level/sales volume/closing stock requirement: These do not usually feature in a production budget but are incorporated here to indicate the basis on which most production requirements are worked out.

Materials/labour/overheads: By unit, by hour and as a proportion of the firm's overhead expenditure, respectively. Note that this business is producing only one item – a convenient over-simplification! Note also that headings and sub-headings will vary from one budget to another.

Est/act/var: 'Estimated', 'actual' and 'variance'. Having three columns allows the budget to be checked at regular intervals and any variations to be spotted promptly and dealt with.

The full budget would have a 'Totals' column at the far right, after the final month of the year.

Figure 1.2   Production budget: a simplified example

Capital expenditure budget

This budget is concerned with estimated expenditure on capital goods during the relevant period of time. 'Capital goods' are those items of permanent, long-term value to the concern. Normally, they will be grouped by type – land, buildings, equipment, machinery and so forth.

Detailed figures justifying the expenditure and indicating when it will be recouped may be included as well. Refer to Figure 1.3 for an example of a straightforward capital expenditure budget.

CAPITAL EXPENDITURE BUDGET 2000	January			February			March		
	Est.	Act.	Var.	Est.	Act.	Var.	Est.	Act.	Var.
Land and buildings: Adjacent wasteland (Harper's Grove) Warehouse unit (Schugardt 164X)	49,000 —			— —			— 38,000		
Total land and buildings (£)	49,000			—			38,000		
Plant, equipment, machinery: 4 x lathes (IBX 4217) 1 x computer system (CBS RIV 2)	— 12,600			— —			88,800 —		
Total plant, equipment, machinery (£)	12,600			—			88,800		
Vehicles: 2 x cars (Vauxhall Cavalier)	—			—			32,000		
Total vehicles (£)	—			—			32,000		
Grand total (£)	61,600			—			158,800		

Land and buildings/plant, equipment, machinery/vehicles: Although all of these are not always relevant, they are included here to show what might be detailed in such a budget. Headings and sub-headings do vary from budget to budget, according to circumstances.

Est/act/var: 'Estimated', 'Actual' and 'Variance'. Kindly note that as capital purchases tend to be fewer and less frequent than others, a more relaxed monitoring system may apply: perhaps on an 'as and when purchased' basis. The underlying principle of regularly reviewing results remains the same though.

A 'Totals' column would be placed to the far right of the complete form.

Figure 1.3   Capital expenditure budget: a straightforward example

Departmental budgets

Budgets for each of the departments – or even sections – within the organisation will have to be drawn up, establishing their respective expenditures for the upcoming period. These are sometimes classified in two ways. 'Operational budgets' are composed for those sections or departments – typically marketing and distribution – whose work is linked with the value of business being achieved. 'Support budgets' are compiled for those which act in a supportive capacity – finance and administration are obvious examples.

Extracts from basic distribution and administration budgets are reproduced as Figures 1.4 and 1.5 respectively. (See page 7.)

DISTRIBUTION BUDGET 2000	January			February			March		
	Est.	Act.	Var.	Est.	Act.	Var.	Est.	Act.	Var.
Drivers' wages	15,000			15,000			15,000		
Fuel and oil	4,000			4,000			4,000		
Tax and insurance	2,700			2,700			2,700		
Vehicle maintenance	2,300			2,300			2,300		
Vehicle repairs	1,500			1,500			3,000		
Vehicle depreciation	10,000			10,000			10,000		
Grand total (£)	35,500			35,500			37,000		

Drivers' wages/fuel and oil/tax and insurance/vehicle maintenance/vehicle repairs/vehicle depreciation: These are typical examples of some of the types of sub-heading to be found in such a budget. They could be divided further in most instances – 'Vehicle repairs' including 'Labour', 'Replacement parts' and so on, for example. Other sub-headings may be equally relevant here, instead of or in addition to those listed.

Est/act/var: Three columns are essential in departmental budgets in particular, as regular checks must begin at the lowest levels of an organisation and work upwards from there.

A 'Totals' column should be incorporated to the far right of the whole form, after 'December'.

Figure 1.4   Distribution budget: an extract

ADMINISTRATION BUDGET 2000	January			February			March		
	Est.	Act.	Var.	Est.	Act.	Var.	Est.	Act.	Var.
Salaries	14,000			14,000			16,000		
Expenses	800			800			1,000		
Postage	500			500			1,000		
Stationery	1,200			1,200			2,300		
Computer maintenance	200			200			250		
Computer depreciation	500			500			500		
Furniture depreciation	500			500			500		
Grand total (£)	17,700			17,700			21,550		

Salaries/expenses/postage/stationery/computer maintenance/computer depreciation/furniture depreciation: These are a selection of the standardised sub-headings likely to be seen in a budget of this kind. Additional ones may be equally appropriate, as might alternatives.

Est/act/var: 'Estimated', 'actual' and 'variance'. It is important that all three columns are put into the budget so continuous monitoring is encouraged to take place.

A 'Totals' column must be placed at the far right of the complete budget.

Figure 1.5   Administration budget: an extract

CASH BUDGET 2000	January			February			March		
Receipts:	*Est.*	*Act.*	*Var.*	*Est.*	*Act.*	*Var.*	*Est.*	*Act.*	*Var.*
Cash sales	47,000			56,000			58,000		
Cash from debtors	5,000			—			—		
Capital introduced	—			—			—		
Total receipts (A)	**52,000**			**56,000**			**58,000**		
Payments:									
Payments to suppliers	26,000			27,000			36,000		
Salaries, wages	8,000			8,000			8,000		
Rent, rates, water	13,000			—			—		
Insurance	—			1,000			—		
Repairs, renewals	—			—			—		
Heat, light, power	—			—			1,200		
Postage	400			400			400		
Printing, stationery	2,000			—			—		
Transport	800			800			800		
Telephone	—			—			500		
Professional fees	—			—			—		
Capital payments	—			—			—		
Interest charges	—			—			—		
Other	—			—			—		
VAT payable	—			16,000			—		
Total payments (B)	**50,200**			**53,200**			**46,900**		
Net cashflow (A–B)	**1,800**			**2,800**			**11,100**		
Opening bank balance	14,600			16,400			19,200		
Closing bank balance	16,400			19,200			30,300		

Receipts/payments: These categories could also be titled 'revenues' and 'expenditure' or 'incomings' and 'outgoings', as preferred by the individual organisation. Sub-categories may be as shown (or similar) or by function, department or section ('finance', 'administration' and so on. Again, this is a matter of choice.

Est/act/var: 'Estimated', 'actual' and 'variance'. The cash position of any business has to be appraised regularly, often more frequently than once each month as suggested. Weekly reviews may be better to avoid potential problems.

A 'Totals' column should be located to the far right of the full budget, after the final month of December.

Figure 1.6   Cash budget: an extract

Master budget

In effect, the master budget summarises all of the preceding budgets, pulling them together to produce three, key documents – a cash budget, a budgeted profit and loss account and a budgeted balance sheet.

A 'cash budget' sets down the on-going cash position of a firm by recording anticipated cash inflows and outflows during the relevant period of time. Look at Figure 1.6 to see an extract from a cash budget.

A 'budgeted profit and loss account' shows a firm's sales revenue over the period in question and all relevant costs incurred in order to generate that revenue, leaving a profit or a loss on trading activities.

A 'budgeted balance sheet' sets out the firm's assets such as equipment, machinery and stocks of raw materials, plus its liabilities like debts to suppliers as at the end of the period. Concise examples of both documents are illustrated in Figures 1.7 and 1.8.

Sales		368,000
Opening stock	65,000	
Purchases	155,000	
Closing stock	60,000	
Cost of sales		160,000
Gross profit		**208,000**
Overheads:		
Salaries	63,000	
Rent, rates, water	15,000	
Insurance	1,600	
Repairs, renewals	1,000	
Heat, light, power	1,200	
Postage	800	
Printing, stationery	2,000	
Transport	1,000	
Telephone	1,300	
Professional fees	1,000	
Interest charges	500	
Depreciation	1,000	
Total		**89,400**
Net profit		**118,600**

Cost of sales: Calculated by taking opening stock *adding* purchases and then *deducting* closing stock.

Gross profit: Sales less cost of sales.

Overheads: These will vary according to the firm. They may be listed by item as shown (or similar) either in a pre-determined or descending order according to the sums spent on them. Alternatively, they can be listed by function, department or section ('marketing', 'personnel' and so forth).

Net profit: Gross profit less overheads.

Figure 1.7   Budgeted profit and loss account: a concise example

Fixed assets:	
Leasehold property	60,000
Equipment	40,000
Vehicles	20,000
	120,000
Current assets:	
Stock	25,000
Debtors	12,000
Cash	5,000
	42,000
Current liabilities:	
Bank loan	16,000
Trade creditors	10,000
Sundry creditors	3,000
	29,000
Net current assets	13,000
Net assets	133,000
Financed by:	
Partners' capital	20,000
Mortgage	50,000
Profit	63,000
	133,000

Fixed assets: Items of permanent use to a business.

Current assets/current liabilities: Ever changing items and/or sums owned or owed, and due to be paid in the next 12 months.

Net current assets: Current assets minus current liabilities.

Net assets: Fixed assets *plus* net current assets.

Financed by: The total should be the same as the net assets thus creating a balance(d) sheet.

Figure 1.8   Budgeted balance sheet: a concise example

The advantages of budgeting

Assuming that budgeting is carried out in a conscientious and effective manner before, during *and* after budgets are set, it will offer numerous benefits both to the organisation and its employees. In particular, the process;

- acts as a plan

- performs a co-ordinating role

- creates a framework

- offers an incentive

- provides a control facility.

A plan

The initial stage of compiling budgets does encourage individuals, departments and the business itself to look ahead and to plan – taking account of all of the circumstances, calculating likely revenues, working out probable expenditure, being aware of the possible influences upon them, and so forth. Clearly, this preliminary planning (and indeed on-going planning as revised and new budgets are drawn up and agreed) is advantageous – not least because it helps to identify the viability of different activities, their likely consequences, cash situations and probable profits or losses well in advance. Thus, you can act *before* rather than react *after* to take advantage of opportunities and to avoid problems.

> Assuming that budgeting is carried out in a conscientious and effective manner before, during *and* after budgets are set, it will offer numerous benefits both to the organisation and its employees.

A co-ordinator

Drafting assorted budgets and then bringing them together within an overall, master budget can help to co-ordinate employees and departments within a firm. Hopefully, everyone knows his or her budget inside out, agrees with it, understands how it fits in with the others and recognises the knock-on effects that will occur if it is surpassed. Budgeting can have a unifying influence with everybody working as part of a team to make sure that they *all* succeed; achieving the required revenues and not exceeding the set expenditure.

A framework

In many respects, budgeting could be said to create a framework for individuals, departments and the business to work within and towards. It sets out the financial responsibilities of supervisors and/or managers, making them answerable for the success or failure of their sections and/or departments. They all understand precisely what they and their teams have to achieve to stay on course. It also quantifies the overall financial objectives of the concern, towards which everyone should be working.

An incentive

Budgeting can motivate people to work harder and do better. In essence, budgets establish the required standards and consequently become goals that need to be reached – to obtain specified revenues *and* by certain dates, to maintain a positive cash position at all times, to keep expenditure within agreed limits, and so on. Obviously, employees are motivated in innumerable ways – and the chance to achieve targets, to be recognised as successful and be praised and congratulated is a powerful incentive.

A control

The later stages of trying to adhere to budgets (and hopefully succeeding) enable individuals, departments and the business to exercise a considerable degree of control over their activities – comparing estimated and actual results, identifying variances and the corrective action needed to remedy them and then taking the action that will allow you to manage the situation; attending to difficulties before it is too late.

The disadvantages of budgeting

Despite its numerous advantages, budgeting does have some disadvantages too – even though you will attempt to minimise these as much as possible, or to eliminate them altogether. More specifically, budgeting can:

- increase paperwork
- be time-consuming

- be inflexible
- meet with resistance
- be slow to work.

Increased paperwork

The introduction of a budgetary system inevitably brings a mass of paperwork with it – before budgets are set, whilst they are being established and afterwards, when they are being monitored and perhaps amended. Although this extra paperwork is necessary – indeed unavoidable – it can sometimes take over, with form after form being completed, studied, revised and so forth whereas attention might be better directed towards the practicalities of selling goods regularly, purchasing at the most competitive prices and the like. It is important that budgeting is seen as a means to an end – not the end itself.

Time-consuming

Even when budgeting is viewed as a means to an end – and therefore kept in proportion – it is still a time-consuming process, particularly at the outset when the system is being developed, tested and refined. Whoever is given overall responsibility for its implementation – typically the finance director or chief accountant – will find it takes up a significant amount of his or her time. Even at departmental level, it will occupy much of the managers' time too – in terms of both activities *and* thoughts. As time progresses though, and if the system is working well, it will require less – albeit fairly regular – work doing on it.

Inflexible

The whole concept of budgeting – revenues to be achieved and by certain dates, expenditure to be kept within specified limits and not exceeded – can seem very inflexible, and restrictive. Obviously, a 'first time around' budget may be inaccurate. Some departments or sections such as research and development are not suited to a rigid budget, whilst others have expenditures linked closely to sales. Sometimes, circumstances change as budgets develop. Thus, it is essential that budgets are not fixed completely but allow room for adjustments to be made, as and when necessary.

Resistance

Too often, budgets are met with resistance, most notably at departmental or sectional level. Many employees regard the implementation of a budgetary system with suspicion, believing it to be little more than a cost-cutting exercise, and perhaps even as a sign of an impending reduction in working hours, redundancy, or whatever. Not surprisingly, this resistance is stronger and more significant when budgets are tight and inflexible.

It is possible to lower – or even remove – any resistance by involving everyone at an early stage when setting budgets. The closer the involvement, the more co-operative employees are likely to be when carrying out the consequent (agreed) activities.

Slow to work

The development of an effective budgetary system does take time – many of the early budgets set will almost certainly have to be amended often *and* substantially, probably because of inexperience and over-optimistic or ultra-cautious judgements being made. As initial mistakes are remedied, learned from and experience is gained, budgets should become much more accurate.

However, as a (very) rough and ready rule of thumb, it will normally take one or two years to set up a reliable system, and have it running effectively.

Budgetary procedures

The budgetary procedures which take place within businesses will vary from one organisation to another. However, most firms will follow a similar series of steps, as highlighted in Figure 1.9. Typically, the sequence is thus:

- sales forecast compiled
- production forecast drafted

- capital expenditure forecast composed
- departmental forecasts drawn up
- budget committee receives forecast
- budget committee sets master budget
- budget committee confirms individual budgets
- variation reports completed regularly
- corrective action identified
- corrective action carried out.

Sales forecast compiled

It is probably wise to distinguish at this point between a forecast and a budget. Although they will to all intents and purposes look the same, a forecast sets out what is likely to happen, be required or whatever, whereas a budget states what *should* occur – or else! Hence, a sales forecast is drawn up by the sales manager and his or her team, and predicts what the sales will probably be over the coming months and year, as appropriate. More often than not, the sales forecast is the first to be compiled simply because the majority of firms base their activities and planned expenditure around their anticipated revenues.

Production forecast drafted

Usually, the production forecast is then composed on the basis of the preceding sales budget forecast. Production capacity – simply the maximum amount that can be produced by a firm over a given period – will be assessed by the production manager and his or her colleagues. Production levels will then be set in relation to estimated sales, whilst taking note of opening stock and the required closing stock levels, which may need to be higher or lower than at the outset. From these figures, direct materials, direct labour and factory overheads can be worked out and allocated, as relevant.

In some instances, the production budget will be drawn up first – most notably when production capacity is limited and sales must be matched to it, rather than vice versa.

Whatever the situation, it is imperative that both sales and production forecasts are compiled in unison and linked together closely.

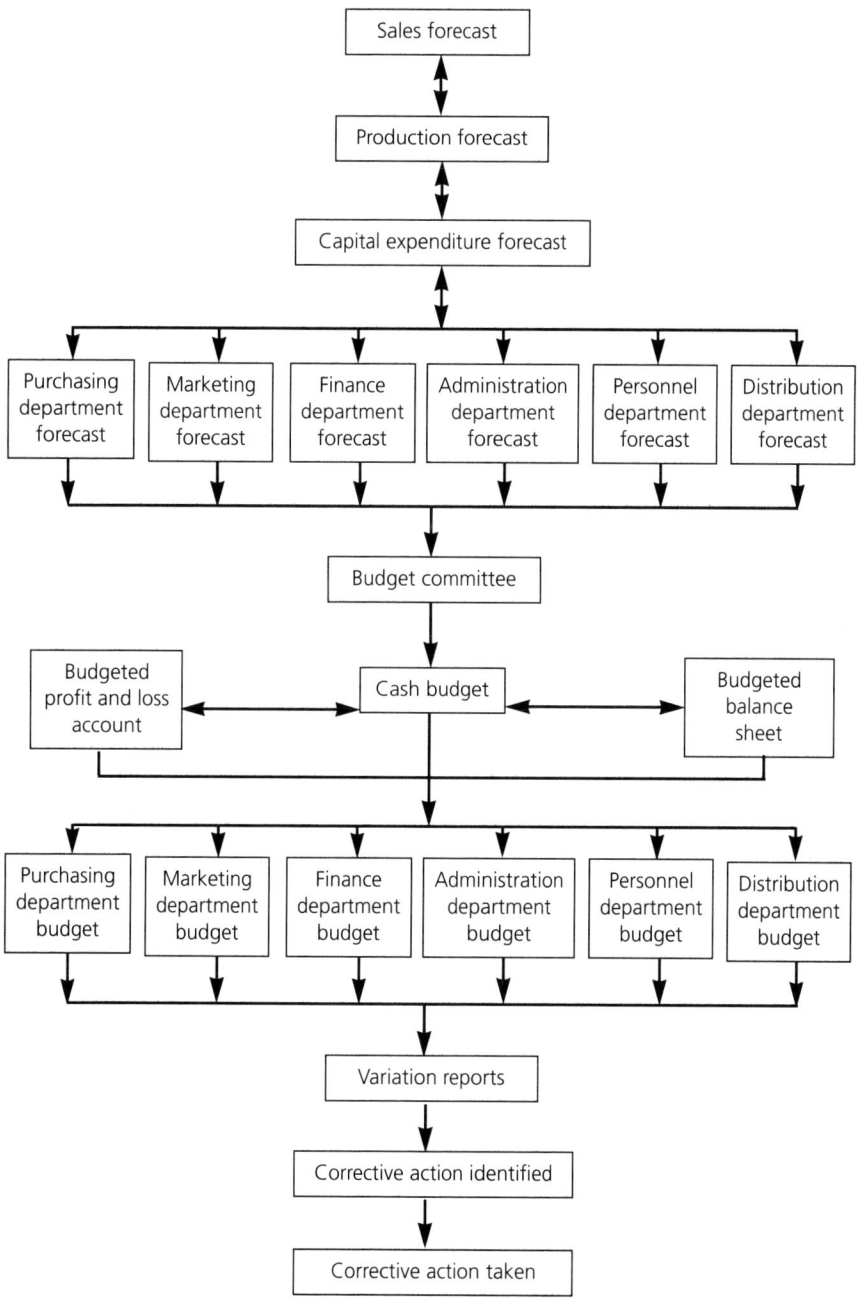

Figure 1.9   Budgetary procedures: a flowchart

Ideally, perhaps sales growth and maximised production capacity will occur. If sales exceed capacity, then additional and costly capital items may be needed. Conversely, if production capacity is not utilised fully, attempts might have to be made to either raise sales or to sell unwanted capital stocks.

Capital expenditure forecast composed

Logically, a capital expenditure forecast will be put together in the light of the sales and production forecasts, taking account of any differences between them which may imply that various capital goods need to be bought or are surplus to requirements. Of course, some items may have to be purchased because of exhausted existing equipment, changing technology and the like, with others being offloaded as appropriate – which will be decided by the finance director or whoever, drawing on information provided by the sales, production and other departmental managers within the firm.

Departmental forecasts drawn up

With the relevant information from the sales and production budget forecasts being made available as necessary, additional budgets will be composed, setting down the revenues and (more likely) the expenditures within the remaining departments – purchasing, marketing, finance, administration, personnel, distribution, or whatever. Not surprisingly, these will be pieced together by the departmental managers and their teams, typically working in close co-operation with each other. Key data concerning capital goods will be passed to the finance department, or whoever is responsible for creating that capital expenditure budget.

Budget committee receives forecasts

In most organisations, all of these forecasts are then submitted to a budget committee which will have been formed simply to vet and consequently approve or amend them, and to draw up a cash budget, budgeted profit and loss account and a budgeted balance sheet. The composition of this committee will vary according to individual circumstances, but might be chaired by the Finance Director or whoever has ultimate responsibility for budgeting within the firm, and have the various departmental managers who compiled the forecasts as its members.

Budget committee sets master budget

Once the numerous budget forecasts have been assessed, the information contained within them will be used to compose the cash budget, budgeted profit and loss account and budgeted balance sheet – in short, the master budget. More often than not, this will be a tough and protracted process as it is improbable that all of the forecasts will instantly gel together well and adjustments will have to be made to them. It is likely that the Finance Director – or whoever has overall charge in this instance – will have the final say in the decision-making process.

Budget committee confirms individual budgets

As soon as the master budget has been agreed, all of the other budgets – sales, production, capital expenditure and departmental ones can be established and confirmed to the appropriate departments. In many cases, either the sales and/or the production budget will be passed without significant adjustment (depending on which one is predominant in the particular situation) whilst the remaining budgets will have to be amended perhaps substantially to fit in with them and indeed, each other. Most departmental budgets are a compromise.

Variation reports completed regularly

To adhere as much as possible to the budgets that have been set, it is necessary for them to be monitored at appropriate intervals. What would be considered 'appropriate' depends on the specific situation and how uncertain it is – a cash budget may need to be checked weekly, a sales budget monthly and an administration budget on a quarterly basis. Variation reports – which simply record the estimated and actual revenues and/or expenditure with any variances noted alongside of them – have to be filled in when major differences exist: typically in excess of 10 per cent. An extract from a variation report is shown as Figure 1.10.

Corrective action identified

Often, only noticeable and/or potentially troublesome variances will be brought to the attention of the relevant departmental manager who will then identify the corrective action needed to remedy the matter – for example, delay payments, chase up outstanding debts or whatever, to improve a poor cashflow situation.

Most organisations now practise this 'management by exception' technique, whereby only important variations are referred to managers, although its success is heavily reliant on a good understanding between management and staff, especially with regard to what is 'important'.

Corrective action carried out

Hopefully, the corrective action that was identified – to delay this, to chase that and so on – will ensure that subsequent estimated and actual figures are closer than before if not the same. Those variances that cannot be remedied and which may have substantial knock-on effects on this and other budgets will need to be passed upwards so that adjustments and allowances can be made. A simplified example of the operation of a budgetary system through to this stage is illustrated in Case Study 1.1, to clarify its basic principles.

Variation Report: Revenues		Period: May 2000			Year to date: August 1999–May 2000			Reason(s) for variance(s)
		Est.	Act.	Var.	Est.	Act.	Var.	
Product GR 27	Volume	200	150	50	3,000	2,850	150	Smaller orders placed than anticipated due to market uncertainty. Expect proportionate increases in next period. No cause for concern.
	Price	100	100	—	100	100	—	
	Value	20,000	15,000	5,000	300,000	285,000	15,000	
Product GR 28	Volume	400	300	100	5,000	4,800	200	Major order from Thompsons not received due to holiday of both partners – to be issued on return. No cause for concern.
	Price	75	75	—	75	75	—	
	Value	30,000	22,500	7,500	375,000	360,000	15,000	
Product BR 31	Volume	300	250	50	5,000	4,700	300	Unexpected closure of Reilly's. Appointments made with other retailers in towns to open new accounts.
	Price	125	125	—	125	125	—	
	Value	37,500	31,250	6,250	625,000	587,500	37,500	
Product BR 32X	Volume	300	250	50	3,000	2,700	300	Unexpected closure of Reilly's. Appointments made with other retailers in towns to open new accounts.
	Price	100	100	—	100	100	—	
	Value	30,000	25,000	5,000	300,000	270,000	30,000	

The first column may be grouped by 'Product', 'Territory', 'Market', 'Type of revenue', 'Other' or whatever is most appropriate in the circumstances.

Volume/price/variance: In units, £ sterling and £ sterling respectively.

Period: To be filled in with the name of the month (or whatever), followed by relevant figures for that time.

Year to date: To be completed with the names of the months covered so far, followed by the cumulative figures for the period.

Est/act/var: 'Estimated', 'actual', 'variance'. These three columns enable variances to be highlighted fully.

Reason(s) for variance(s): To be suggested, along with suggestions for proposed corrective action, if appropriate.

The complete form would have 'Department', 'Date', 'Name' and 'Signature' boxes (or similar) at the bottom.

Another form for expenditure variances might be available too, with expenditure divided up according to company preferences.

Figure 1.10   Variation report: an extract

CASE STUDY 1.1   **The operation of a budgetary system**

Steve and Cathy own and run a small but growing company – Newbabes Limited – in East Anglia. Started in 1993 from their large country house, they manufacture and sell innovative baby changing bags through the retail trade to prospective and existing parents. In 1996 – with sales restricted by a low production capacity – Steve and Cathy had a purpose-built factory unit erected in their grounds. Production and sales rose substantially and they now employ a workforce of some 70 people headed by a management team of three.

Raj, Mary and Adam are responsible for personnel, marketing and distribution respectively. Steve is in charge of purchasing and production, and Cathy handles the day-to-day financial and administrative activities – between them, they also oversee the three managers, albeit almost nominally in most instances. Everyone works together as a team, advising and helping each other as and when necessary. In many respects, Newbabes is a model small business. Indeed, it celebrated 1998 with a small business award.

Budgeting for the 1998–9 accounting year commenced formally some six months before the beginning of the period (although in reality it was part of a permanent, on-going programme of financial planning and control without specified start and end dates). At one of their regular weekly management meetings, Steve and Cathy asked Mary to prepare a sales forecast for the period, which she subsequently did – see Case study 2.1 (pages 37–8) for further details. Simultaneously, Steve calculated the firm's current production capacity – a worry from earlier years – and they then liaised at a meeting two weeks later.

Although the anticipated sales were within production capacity capabilities, it was agreed by everyone that current levels of production should be raised some 10 per cent above those needed to satisfy sales demand in order to increase stock levels. Adam in particular felt that likely ordering patterns linked to seasonal highs and lows meant that more back-up stocks were needed – they had run short in previous years which had harmed delivery schedules and consequently, sales and the company's reputation. With this in mind, Steve went away to prepare a production budget forecast – refer to Case study 2.2 (pages 45–6) for more explanation.

At this same meeting, Mary and Steve agreed that no new capital items were needed to maintain the expected sales and production levels, although there were indications that some equipment might be required elsewhere. Cathy was responsible for drawing up a capital expenditure budget forecast and said she would look into this – see Case study 2.3 (pages 47–8) for more information. Everyone then also agreed to compile what could be termed departmental – or in this instance 'functional' – forecasts for personnel, marketing, distribution, finance and administration. Raj had the biggest task to do, for personnel – as detailed in Case study 3.1 (page 65).

Two weeks on, the five managers formed what might be described as a budget committee, headed by Cathy. All of the various forecasts were presented by the appropriate people, worked through, explained and discussed. As the team had referred to each other constantly during compilation of the forecasts, they were largely in agreement about their respective requirements – a quite unusual occurrence! Assuming the forecasts fitted together well, they should be passed as budgets. To verify this, Cathy took away the accumulated information in order to compile a cash budget, budgeted profit and loss account and budgeted balance sheet – see Case studies 4.1 (page 81) and 4.2 (pages 103–5) for more details.

Satisfied with the completed master budget – which showed healthy cash surpluses and profits throughout the period – Cathy circulated copies of the relevant documents to the managers. She confirmed that the forecasts – with one or two amendments primarily regarding the timings of various expenditure – had been approved and accorded budget status. Some of these amendments were raised and talked over at a subsequent meeting with agreement being reached and the budgets remaining the same.

The 1998–9 budgets were monitored by the relevant managers – Raj for personnel, Mary for marketing and so on. Due to the size of the firm and its centralised organisation, each manager was conscious of his or her budget on a daily basis with informal comments and discussions being raised as necessary at the weekly meetings. The managers completed the appropriate sections of their budgets – namely the 'actual' and 'variance' columns – every month, as can be seen in Case studies 5.1 (pages 117–18) and 5.2 (page 121). The subsequent management meeting was then used to talk through any significant variances.

Bearing in mind the experience of the managers involved in setting budgets and the close control which was exercised after that, difficulties were few and far between. The only two of significance were lower sales than anticipated during a seasonal lull and lengthier payment times, most notably by a new, major purchaser. Suggestions to resolve these problems were put forward during meetings and acted upon effectively, as illustrated in Case studies 6.1 (page 130) and 6.2 (pages 134–5). Some changes did have to be made to relevant budgets – see Case study 6.3 (page 140).

Newbabes' 1998–9 year ended successfully, with all managers completing their budgets satisfactorily and the overall master budget being almost wholly accurate. Towards the end of the period – and in accordance with their rolling programme of planning and control – Steve, Cathy, Raj, Mary and Adam looked towards the 1999–2000 year and decided it would be a good idea to investigate the possibility of diversification into a range of complementary and equally innovative nursery goods. Market research commenced …

SUMMARY

1 Budgeting is the process of compiling budgets and subsequently adhering to them as closely as possible.

2 A budget is a financial plan that sets out anticipated revenues and/or estimated expenditure over a forthcoming period of time, typically one year. Numerous budgets are drawn up within a business:

(a) sales budget

(b) production budget

(c) capital expenditure budget

(d) departmental budgets

(e) master budget

3 Budgeting offers numerous advantages both to the organisation and its employees:

(a) it acts as a plan

(b) it performs a co-ordinating role

(c) it creates a framework

(d) it offers an incentive

(e) it provides a control facility

4 Budgeting does have some disadvantages too:

(a) it increases paperwork

(b) it is time-consuming

(c) it can be inflexible

(d) it can meet with resistance

(e) it is slow to work

5 Budgetary procedures vary from one business to another, although most will follow a similar series of steps:

(a) sales forecast compiled

(b) production forecast drafted

(c) capital expenditure forecast composed

(d) departmental forecasts drawn up

(e) budget committee receives forecasts

(f) budget committee sets master budget

(g) budget committee confirms individual budgets

(h) variation reports completed regularly

(i) corrective action identified

(j) corrective action carried out

Your all-important, preparatory work for budgeting success consists of three main stages – gathering information, anticipating revenues and estimating expenditure.

How to prepare budget forecasts

- Gathering information

- Anticipating revenues

- Estimating expenditure

- Summary

With a broader understanding of the budgetary process, you can move on to prepare a budget forecast, whether for sales, production, capital expenditure or your own particular department.

Your all-important, preparatory work for budgeting success consists of three main stages – gathering information, anticipating revenues and estimating expenditure. Each stage is of equal significance and should be paid the same amount of attention.

Gathering information

The background information that you need to accumulate and how and where you obtain it will vary according to your individual requirements and circumstances. Nevertheless, there are some common areas which are applicable to most situations:

- the limiting factor
- external influences
- internal influences
- sources of advice.

The limiting factor

Although it sounds rather theoretical, the idea of a 'limiting factor' is a very real and practical one. The phrase simply refers to a key, overriding influence which has a significant, constraining effect upon all relevant budgets. For example, a small and stagnant marketplace will act as a limit on potential sales which will in turn have knock-on effects on consequent budgets. Similarly, a scarcity of raw materials may be a limiting factor on production levels – and therefore upon the sales, capital expenditure and departmental budgets too. Obviously, sales and the equipment and labour required will all be affected adversely if production is restricted.

You need to identify for yourself what the limiting factor(s) is/are in your company, and specific situation.

Perhaps there is a lack of funds available for expanding sales and/or production levels, purchasing new capital items and so on. Possibly, a shortage of labour or up-to-date equipment and machinery will affect production and subsequent budgets. A checklist of typical limiting factors is shown as Figure 2.1 – see which ones are applicable to you.

Most companies' budgets will be drawn up with a 'limiting factor' in mind – something which constrains each and every one of them, either directly or indirectly. These are some of the more common ones:

■ the objectives stated in the memorandum of association, which the company is legally obliged to adhere.

■ a lack of finance for investment in the firm's activities.

■ a scarce or irregular supply of raw materials, component parts or goods for resale.

■ a shortage of labour, typically of a particular, skilled nature.

■ a lack of up-to-date equipment and machinery.

■ a leasehold agreement, forbidding activities in certain areas.

■ an absence of planning permission to diversify into other areas.

■ a lack of alternative sites for relocation and development.

■ incomplete knowledge and understanding about a new market.

■ a small and stagnant marketplace, with a limited customer base.

■ rivals' anti-competitive practices, restricting entry into and/or activities in a market.

■ a monopolistic marketplace, dominated by one or two large and powerful competitors.

■ competition laws preventing a monopoly situation from developing.

■ quotas on imports and exports coming into and going out of a country.

Figure 2.1   Limiting factors: a checklist

External influences

Conscious of this overall constraint upon your sales, production, capital expenditure, departmental budget or whatever, you should contemplate and list for future reference all of the possible, (other) external influences which may also have some effect on your particular budget, and its revenues and expenditure.

Again, these will depend on your given situation but might include rivals' products, activities and strategies plus economic factors such as inflation and interest rates. Figure 2.2 indicates some of the numerous external factors that may be of relevance in your circumstances.

Here is a list of some of the possible external influences upon your budget. You may find it helpful to tick those which are relevant to you. Then think carefully about how your budget might be affected by them, for better or worse.

	Relevant	Irrelevant
Customers:		
types	☐	☐
number	☐	☐
location	☐	☐
wants	☐	☐
needs	☐	☐
levels of demand	☐	☐
Suppliers:		
types	☐	☐
number	☐	☐
location	☐	☐
costs of supply	☐	☐
levels of supply	☐	☐
terms	☐	☐
conditions	☐	☐
Competitors:		
types	☐	☐
number	☐	☐
location	☐	☐
products	☐	☐
activities	☐	☐
strategies	☐	☐
Labour:		
types	☐	☐
number	☐	☐
location	☐	☐
demands	☐	☐
expectations	☐	☐
Population:		
types	☐	☐
number	☐	☐
location	☐	☐
births	☐	☐
deaths	☐	☐
migration	☐	☐
Community:		
neighbours	☐	☐
pressure groups	☐	☐
social trends	☐	☐
cultural trends	☐	☐
the environment	☐	☐

	Relevant	Irrelevant
Government:		
types	☐	☐
competition policy	☐	☐
fiscal policy	☐	☐
industrial policy	☐	☐
monetary policy	☐	☐
Economy:		
structure	☐	☐
cycle	☐	☐
inflation rates	☐	☐
interest rates	☐	☐
taxation levels	☐	☐
Legislation:		
consumer protection	☐	☐
employment laws	☐	☐
health and safety	☐	☐
competition laws	☐	☐
Influential bodies:		
Inland Revenue	☐	☐
Customs and Excise	☐	☐
regulatory organisations	☐	☐
representative associations	☐	☐
landlords	☐	☐
creditors	☐	☐
debtors	☐	☐
media	☐	☐
Europe:		
exports	☐	☐
imports	☐	☐
exchange rates	☐	☐
tariffs	☐	☐
taxes	☐	☐
quotas	☐	☐
European Union	☐	☐
Others (as relevant to your company	☐	☐
	☐	☐

Figure 2.2   External influences on a budget: a checklist

Internal influences

You should be aware of all the (other) internal influences that exist within your section, department and business – and which may have a beneficial or adverse effect upon your upcoming budget and its figures.

Such items as employees' wage demands, stock level requirements and – perhaps most appropriate of all – fellow budgets are often noted down in managers' lists. Various internal influences are set out as Figure 2.3 (on page 32) – some of them will almost certainly be relevant to your situation.

Sources of advice

As you think about those limiting factors, external and internal influences that are most applicable to you, it will become evident (if it was not already) that you do need to have a broad knowledge and understanding of what is going on around you now *and* during the forthcoming period. Only then can you hope to produce a relatively accurate budget forecast that takes account of all of the key circumstances. Accordingly, you will have to draw regularly on the numerous sources of advice available to you.

Internally, this means attending meetings ('What are our objectives?' 'What is happening?') and talking to directors, shareholders, colleagues and employees as and when possible. ('Are dividends to be paid this year?' 'What will the wage levels be?') It also involves reading (between the lines of) memoranda, reports and other documents rather than skimming them, or putting them to one side. ('What new goods are being introduced?' 'What will their prices be?') You have to keep your eyes and ears open permanently, soaking up what is occurring now *and* all the ifs, buts and maybes of what could take place in the future.

Externally, there is even more that can be done, largely because of the greater range and diversity of influences that exist. Chat to customers and suppliers, in particular. ('What are your trading plans for the next year?' 'What discounts are available for larger orders?') Obtain competitors' literature, perhaps by subscribing to their mailing lists if you can. ('Are new products to be launched?' 'Are they selling at lower prices than ours?') Approach trade bodies, reading their newsletters and attending their confer- ences, seminars and exhibitions. ('How will the new code of conduct affect us?' 'What else is going on in the marketplace?')

Here is a list of some of the probable internal influences on your budget. Tick those which are of significance to you and consider fully how your budget will be influenced by them, for good or bad.

	Significant	Insignificant		Significant	Insignificant
Objectives:			stock levels	☐	☐
short term	☐	☐	promotion techniques	☐	☐
medium term	☐	☐	channels of distribution	☐	☐
long term	☐	☐			
			Resources:		
Influential groups:			capital	☐	☐
directors	☐	☐	profits	☐	☐
shareholders	☐	☐	land	☐	☐
unions	☐	☐	buildings	☐	☐
employees	☐	☐	equipment	☐	☐
			machinery	☐	☐
Departments:					
sales	☐	☐	**Budgets:**		
production	☐	☐	sales	☐	☐
purchasing	☐	☐	production	☐	☐
marketing	☐	☐	capital		
finance	☐	☐	expenditure	☐	☐
administration	☐	☐	purchasing	☐	☐
personnel	☐	☐	marketing	☐	☐
others	☐	☐	finance	☐	☐
			administration	☐	☐
Goods and services:			personnel	☐	☐
types	☐	☐	others	☐	☐
number	☐	☐			
production methods	☐	☐	**Others (as relevant to your**		
prices	☐	☐	**company**	☐	☐
pricing methods	☐	☐			

Figure 2.3   Internal influences on a budget: a checklist

Read more widely – general and business newspapers and magazines, for example. ('Are inflation rates expected to rise?' 'What about interest rates?') Get hold of more specific documents as well – such as government and European Union publications ('How is the population changing?' 'What European directives and legislation are being passed?') A whole host of other advisory individuals and organisations can be contacted too – business consultants, job centres, employment agencies and local authorities amongst them. Be careful though – it is tempting to pursue your knowledge and understanding to extreme lengths, *thinking* rather than doing! Know enough to make educated guesses and where to go for a second opinion – that should be sufficient.

Anticipating revenues

Knowing about any limiting factors and potential external and internal influences that exist, you can set about anticipating your probable revenues over the budgetary period – if appropriate in your circumstances.

It is sensible to make notes by working through three stages:

- types
- amounts
- timings.

Types

Obviously, the types of revenue that are likely to be obtained will depend on the budget for which you are responsible. For a sales budget, it will mainly – if not wholly – be income from goods and services sold. You should divide this into various sub-headings – perhaps by product group, sales representatives' territory or marketplace. This will consequently make it that much easier to monitor and analyse properly, *and* to make changes as and where relevant. It is up to you to decide how far to sub-divide – far enough to produce meaningful figures, but not so far that you become over-involved with excessive data.

Of course, other types of revenue may be significant too, especially for budgets like production, capital expenditure and departmental ones such as personnel, finance and administration. For example, an injection of capital – from an incoming partner or share issue perhaps – may be allocated to marketing's research and development section to investigate the viability of a proposed new product, diversification into another market, or whatever. Likewise, the sale of unwanted capital items – surplus to requirements because the firm has moved into new ones – could produce funds which are re-allocated to the appropriate department, or section even.

Whatever types of revenue are applicable in your situation – and you may well be able to think of more – it is important that they are always headed and sub-headed in the same way throughout the company.

This will ensure that the various – often quite diverse – budgets are composed along familiar lines and everyone can understand and comment on each other's. It also makes it easier for the documents comprising the master budget to be pieced together with a greater degree of accuracy.

Amounts

Sales income can be hard to predict – both in terms of quantities and prices.

To estimate quantities, you need to start at the lowest level, and build upwards from there.

Ask each sales representative to calculate every one of their customers' probable purchases over the coming budgetary period. Inevitably, they will produce figures for you which have been based – to varying degrees – on customers' previous purchasing records, recent comments and promises, the representative's knowledge of forthcoming products and developments, their views of likely customer reactions and gut feelings (which is unfortunate but unavoidable, however much you stress the need to be objective).

You then need to question representatives one at a time about their figures. (What makes you think that so-and-so will buy that much? Why will such and such a company purchase 20 per cent more this year than last? Why have you put this figure down, and not that?) Draw your own conclusions about these figures, taking particular note of past performances, the representatives' (cautious or optimistic) natures and reasons *plus* your knowledge of those external and internal influences. As an example, you may be aware that one representative is due to retire and his territory to be divided up between other representatives – with favourable or unfavourable repercussions on sales.

Hopefully, the prices of goods and services sold will be easier to calculate – especially if you have a price list to refer to! Take note of any discounts available as well, for prompt payment, bulk buys or whatever, studying payment records to date and anticipated purchases to work out the overall effects on prices of such discounts. Talk to those responsible for setting prices, terms and conditions within your company to see if any rises and/or changes are due to be implemented at a set time of the forthcoming year as usually occurs, *and* what these are likely to be. Think over your understanding of external and internal factors – falling customer demand, increased profit objectives, perhaps – before amending your calculations accordingly.

You should find it relatively straightforward to reach informed estimates about the various amounts of other revenues anticipated during the period, such as capital injections from new partners, shareholders or the sale of capital items. Data about the number of incoming partners, shares to be issued and equipment and machinery to be cleared out should be readily available from meetings, discussions and by simply being aware of what is going on around you. Have your own ideas though, allowing for those external and internal influences – forthcoming bad media publicity may deter one or two partners from joining, one director's off the record comments may be overruled by the next month's board meeting and so on.

The actual sums to be obtained from incoming partners, a shares issue or the sale of capital stocks may be more debatable. Once more, some information should be fairly accessible by going along to meetings, talking to people and reading internal documents that are circulated. In the case of capital items' resale values, some external research – speaking to customers, suppliers, trade bodies and the like – should produce minimum and maximum, potential figures. Contemplate those external and internal factors too. For example, a good annual report may have a positive impact on share prices.

Timings

As important as the types and amounts of revenue that will be coming in during the period in question is *when* they will be received – after all, many (albeit usually smaller) businesses fail not because they have low sales and/or trade unprofitably but as a direct result of poor cashflow. Expenditure is continually paid before revenues arrive, until the cash eventually runs out and the firm is forced to cease trading. Even in large concerns with greater financial reserves, it is essential that revenues are obtained as early as possible *and* when expected so that the most efficient use of resources is made.

With regard to sales income, you must be very realistic – if not pessimistic – about payment dates, ignoring your set credit terms in particular. Often, the majority of customers do not adhere to these.

Liaising with your accounts section about payment records to date should give you an outline of probable patterns for the coming period. Speak to sales representatives to draw on their knowledge and opinions – one customer's fortunes look set to improve, another's to worsen, and so forth. Remember to question them carefully about their views.

(So why will so-and-so then pay earlier? Why will another customer start delaying payments?) Mull over external and internal influences too – such as the imminent introduction of a revised discount structure, and its effects.

With regard to sales income, you must be very realistic – if not pessimistic – about payment dates, ignoring your set credit terms in particular. Often, the majority of customers do not adhere to these.

The timings of capital injections should be more reliable, and easier to budget for with partnership agreement, share issue and capital stock sale dates being well known within the company – as before, you just need to keep abreast of what is happening by participating in meetings, chatting to directors and colleagues and perusing memoranda and other documents that come your way. Be conscious of those various external and internal factors – such as the expected closure of a main rival whose equipment may be auctioned off, thus affecting the selling price of your capital items. Case study 2.1 shows how to compile notes for a sales budget forecast. You may find it helpful.

CASE STUDY 2.1   **Compiling notes for a sales budget forecast**

Mary, the marketing manager at Newbabes Limited, manufacturers of an innovative baby changing bag, was asked to produce a sales forecast for the firm's 1998–9 trading period. She agreed to have this ready for presentation to a management meeting, two weeks after the request was made. From discussions with her colleagues, she knew that the overriding limiting factor was the company's production capacity. This had been a severe problem in the early years of the business and could be again if sales were to escalate. If this seemed likely, additional factory space, equipment and trained staff would be required. Steve, co-owner and in charge of production, promised to calculate existing capacity, giving data to Mary as soon as he had the figures.

The first action that Mary took towards producing her forecast was to jot down all the external influences she could think of that might possibly affect it in some way. Mary was most conscious of a number of competitors who had entered the market recently, with similarly-priced but inferior goods. She was also aware that the customer base was changing rapidly – with the marketplace becoming dominated by three or four large multiple retailers and independent traders reducing steadily in numbers. Mary appreciated that continued success in this field would depend substantially upon these multiples' custom. When writing out her list of external factors, she also added some internal influences too. In particular, Mary knew that the main aim of the company for this year was to consolidate – maintaining sales volumes and raising prices in line with inflation – whilst investigating the possibility of producing similar products for alternative markets or to diversify into other goods for this one. She felt that significant growth – with those knock-on effects on space, equipment and staff requirements – would not be welcomed. To bolster sales in the face of competitors' activities, a robust promotional campaign, had been discussed which would feature repackaged goods plus point of sales display units and materials for distribution to and use by retailers.

Mary checked out her thoughts about these specific key influences by obtaining rival companies' products, looking at their sales literature and talking through their likely impact with experienced contacts in the trade. She met the buyers of the main multiples and debated the future of the independent sector with the appropriate representative body – all of which helped to clarify (and largely confirm) her opinions. She discussed the firm's plans with the owners – Steve and Cathy – who indicated that they

▶

did not wish to be totally dependent on one product for much longer and were seeking to spread their risks by developing a broader range some time during 1999–2000. Mary was also given a figure for the promotional campaign which she was to organise and administer.

Armed with this accumulated knowledge, Mary then pressed ahead to compile notes for use with her sales budget forecast. She decided to divide sales income into eight sub-headings – one for each of the four major, multiple customers with the remainder covering the independent sector in the north, east, west and south of the country. In previous years, the forecast had been divided up into 12 geographical regions encompassing both types of retailer but this did not really provide a full and accurate picture of what was happening now, especially the shift to centralised purchasing by the multiples and the diminishing relevance of independent traders.

Mary estimated the likely volume of sales per multiple and region each month in various ways. Most notably, and because orders always came direct from customers rather than via representatives, she began by studying purchasing patterns to date. Whilst being aware that these would not be reproduced again – especially in such changing circumstances – they did give her an idea of the possible volumes to be bought, by whom and approximately when. It provided a broad overview, if nothing else. From this, she checked out orders (and promises of orders) for the forthcoming period, comparing these figures against those from earlier periods. She talked informally to the multiples' buyers, a cross-section of independent retailers and numerous sales agents out on the road whom she knew personally. From this, she felt she could make informed estimates, mindful of those influences at the same time.

Obviously, Mary was aware of the firm's prices for its goods as well as its bulk buy discounts which she was careful to take account of in her estimates of sales values, particularly for the four multiples. Prompt payment discounts were available too and she allowed for these when calculating the timings of payments – again, basing her workings on last year's figures whilst taking into consideration updated information from her talks with buyers, independents and agents. Various external and internal influences were thought of too, such as prices rising in line with inflation at an agreed, later date. Mary was then ready to turn her notes into a sales budget forecast …

Estimating expenditure

To start with, you need to jot down notes about your likely expenditure during the budgetary period – which will be of primary concern to you, whatever your budget.

Again, it is wise to do this in three stages:

- types
- amounts
- timings.

Types

Whether you are composing a production, capital expenditure or departmental budget forecast for finance, administration and the like, there are various types of expenditure that might apply to your circumstances.

> 'Direct' expenditure is that which varies directly with production and/or sales levels, and incorporates costs for items such as raw materials, component parts, goods for resale, labour and after-sales service.

If accurate planning, monitoring and controlling are to be carried out, it is advisable to divide expenditure into at least four types – 'start up', 'direct', 'indirect' and 'capital' expenditure.

However, you are – as always – dependent largely upon what is deemed appropriate in your company.

'Start up' expenditure – as the name implies – encompasses those costs that are incurred purely as a consequence of doing, producing or selling something for the first time. Introducing a new product is an obvious example of this. So, too, would be moving into another market sector to trade. Thus, these expenses might include producing drawings and specifications for that new item, establishing a production line, rewriting and reprinting sales brochures, catalogues and so on. In effect, any 'one-off' costs could fit under this broad heading.

'Direct' expenditure is that which varies directly with production and/or sales levels, and incorporates costs for items such as raw materials, component parts, goods for resale, labour and after-sales service. Basically, if production and/or sales levels rise, then so do direct costs as more of these items are used up too – and vice versa when production and/or sales levels fall. Direct costs are also often known as 'variable' ones.

'Indirect' expenditure covers all of those costs which are incurred by a business on a regular basis, but are not linked directly to production and/or sales. Thus, these will include expenditure on rent, rates, water and so forth. However many products are being manufactured and services provided, these costs will still have to be paid (although, of course, many firms will try to reduce them in some way if sales in particular fall below acceptable levels). Sometimes, indirect costs are referred to as 'fixed costs' or 'overheads'.

'Capital' expenditure – somewhat obviously – is expenditure on non-consumable items of long-term, permanent use to a business. Buildings, plant, equipment, machinery and vehicles can be classified in this way. Most firms will set a threshold figure of perhaps £500, above which items will be classified as capital expenditure, and below which they will be categorised under another heading, such as overheads. Not surprisingly, capital items will depreciate in value, with time and usage.

> 'Indirect' expenditure covers all of those costs which are incurred by a business on a regular basis, but are not linked directly to production and/or sales.

As with the different types of revenue, you need to decide for yourself how (and indeed how far) you are going to sub-divide these four categories – obviously, it will depend mainly on your own circumstances and the costs that are most likely to be incurred in your budget. It is also essential that the headings and sub-headings used are the same throughout the organisation in order to avoid confusion, especially when the master budget is consequently pulled together. Figure 2.4 is a checklist of these headings and numerous sub-headings, some of which should apply to you.

Amounts

You need to contemplate expenditure both in terms of quantities and prices paid. Start-up costs associated with a new project are often the hardest to calculate. Evidently, you need to work out – primarily by liaising with colleagues and employees – exactly what is likely to be involved in this. Potentially, your list of activities and prospective costs may be almost endless. Going back to each department, section and employee as appropriate, you must then ask them to suggest the probable quantities needed and prices to

> 'Capital' expenditure – somewhat obviously – is expenditure on non-consumable items of long-term, permanent use to a business.

It can be useful to have a list of the main expenditure headings and sub-headings that may apply to your budget. Read through the following, marking off those that are relevant, or not:

	Relevant	Irrelevant		Relevant	Irrelevant
Start-up expenditure:			insurance	☐	☐
drawings	☐	☐	repairs, maintenance	☐	☐
specifications	☐	☐	postage	☐	☐
production line	☐	☐	printing	☐	☐
rewriting literature	☐	☐	stationery	☐	☐
reprinting literature	☐	☐	advertising, promotion	☐	☐
other:	☐	☐	telephone	☐	☐
other:	☐	☐	transport	☐	☐
other:	☐	☐	professional fees	☐	☐
			finance charges	☐	☐
Direct expenditure:			other:	☐	☐
raw materials	☐	☐	other:	☐	☐
component parts	☐	☐	other:	☐	☐
goods for resale	☐	☐			
labour wages	☐	☐	**Capital expenditure:**		
after-sales service	☐	☐	buildings	☐	☐
other:	☐	☐	plant	☐	☐
other:	☐	☐	equipment		
other:	☐	☐	machinery	☐	☐
			vehicles	☐	☐
Indirect expenditure:			other:	☐	☐
rent	☐	☐	other:	☐	☐
rates	☐	☐	other:	☐	☐
water	☐	☐			
heat, light, power	☐	☐			

Figure 2.4 Types of expenditure: a checklist

be paid plus total figures for the different costs. Without doubt, their calculations will be based on their previous experiences in comparable situations, current knowledge and, unavoidably, gut feelings.

Work through the various figures given to you in turn. ('Why will this number of catalogues have to be printed?' 'What makes you think it will cost that much?') Come to your own decisions about the reliability of your colleagues' and employees' comments, after listening to their reasons, thinking about their (positive or negative) natures and checking what they have to say, perhaps by obtaining second opinions from outsiders. Contemplate your list of possible external and internal influences too –

perhaps the skills required to operate new technology are in short supply, and increasingly costly.

Direct costs tend to be easier to estimate than start-up expenditure because they are related so closely to the sales (and consequent production) levels that have been established.

Thus, to calculate the quantities of raw materials, component parts and so forth that are likely to be needed for the period, you should refer to the relevant budgets in order to note down these figures. From there, it should be a relatively straightforward task to look at production and labour records to date to evaluate the quantities of direct materials, labour and equipment used at these levels of production. Mull over external and internal factors as well – maybe stock level requirements need to be higher or lower at the end of the period.

Similarly, it is simple enough to anticipate the prices to be paid for certain quantities of direct materials, labour and so on – by checking recent purchasing documents such as tenders, invoices and receipts plus personnel records including departmental, sectional and individual pay forms and slips. Obviously, you have to take account of the varying prices at different levels of sales and output, allowing for bulk buy discounts, overtime rates and so forth. Budget for external and internal influences as usual – for example, seasonal shortages of raw materials and upcoming strikes by overseas dock workers when you are awaiting supplies of imported component parts will be detrimental.

You should be able to estimate most indirect expenditure with considerable ease – all things being equal, your consumption will probably not vary much from one year to the next. Talk to colleagues and employees and refer back to previous expenditure documents and records to give you a firm idea of corresponding outgoings for the forthcoming period of time. Be especially conscious here of external and internal factors, though, which can have a noticeable impact – such as the introduction of more stringent health and safety guidelines for your industry, which may necessitate additional repairs to and maintenance of your premises.

The actual sums handed over for indirect expenditure should be readily identifiable well in advance too – some such as rent will be fixed, whilst others like electricity and gas for heat, light and power can be calculated by looking at the respective unit costs for the preceding period, allowing for any expected increases due and then working out the overall costs in relation to the units used. Obviously, you do need to liaise with landlords, local authorities, suppliers of utilities and the like beforehand. Again, be aware of external and internal influences – the opportunity to obtain electricity, gas and telephone supplies from other, more competitively priced sources may arise, for example.

Capital expenditure on items such as equipment, machinery and vehicles will almost definitely be the easiest to estimate because these goods are bought infrequently and planned for many months or more likely years ahead. Chat to fellow departmental heads, study investment appraisal and depreciation figures for items purchased some time ago and see which have been scheduled for replacement in this period. Pay extra attention to those external and internal factors here – rapidly developing technology, increased sales and production demands, misuse by staff and the introduction of new goods can all affect capital stock requirements.

The prices that will need to be paid for these various items can be ascertained via elementary research – contacting trade bodies, talking to suppliers, obtaining sales literature and negotiating possible deals, for example. Take account of possible price changes between now and the scheduled purchase date, possibly in 11 months' time towards the close of the firm's accounting period. Make allowance for those numerous influences again – overseas imports and new technology which might lower the price of the item you currently require, and increased demand which might lead to price rises.

Timings

The timings of start-up, direct, indirect and capital expenditure must be planned carefully so that it co-ordinates well with the amounts and timings of your incoming revenues.

In short, you must ensure that expenditure does not precede revenues unless absolutely necessary. If such a situation is allowed to persist, the business will encounter the considerable risk of running out of cash and perhaps even being forced to close, despite any underlying profitability.

The smaller the firm and the fewer the resources, the likelier this is to happen.

Inevitably, start-up expenditure will be incurred before any revenues can be recouped from the new product, diversification or whatever. You should work closely with colleagues and employees in research and development or wherever to decide what needs to be paid out when, questioning them thoroughly to conclude which payments can be delayed, what the consequences might be, and so forth. Paying out as little and as late as possible may be a wise approach in many circumstances. Look down your list of external and internal factors to see if any are relevant – as examples, generous prompt payment discounts or forthcoming price increases may encourage earlier rather than later payments.

The timing of direct expenditure on raw materials, component parts, labour or whatever tends to be more predictable as you will know what you require and when by looking at your sales and production figures and working backwards from them. Referring to those documents which detail suppliers' payment terms and conditions, your usual payment times, employees' pay days and so on, you should be able to assess payment dates with some degree of accuracy. Likewise, indirect expenditure on rent, rates, water and similar costs should be easy to schedule, with rent due perhaps quarterly, rates and water rates payable over monthly instalments, and so forth. Be conscious of any appropriate influences – a revised incentive scheme may bring forward some payments to a disgruntled workforce.

Not surprisingly, capital expenditure will often be the simplest to timetable into the budget forecast, because it will have been planned so far in advance in many instances. You need to speak to other departmental heads and check out documents such as investment appraisal forms to establish probable purchasing dates. External and internal factors may be most influential here though – for example, imminent techno-logical developments may make it wise to delay a purchase. Case studies 2.2 and 2.3 are cover making notes for production and capital expenditure budgets. You should find them helpful.

Making notes for a production budget forecast

Co-owner of 'Newbabes', Steve, was in charge of production and responsible for preparing the appropriate budget forecast for the 1998–9 trading year. Initially, production capacity had been put forward as a probable limiting factor upon the firm's activities, but once Steve had checked this, and then ascertained that sales would be within its capabilities, it was no longer considered to be an issue – at least for the time being. However, Steve was conscious of a key, limiting factor upon his budget forecast – namely that it was expected to shadow Mary's sales forecast with production levels set at 10 per cent above those needed to cover sales, in order that stock levels would rise to allow for seasonal highs and lows in demand.

Next, Steve took account of all possible external influences upon his budget forecast and its contents – essentially materials, labour and the equipment and machinery used during production. Amongst the various influences noted, he identified two of particular concern. One supplier of raw materials imported them from a country which was currently in the news because of its changing political situation and worsening economic conditions. This made Steve feel unsure about the availability and costs of future supplies from this source. Another supplier of component parts had recently started to deliver orders later than usual and, according to Cathy, was demanding payment much earlier and more vigorously than before. Steve suspected they were in financial difficulties which worried him too.

Internally, there were numerous influences – as indeed there always are for all budgets – but the main one concerned the workforce's pay demands. Traditionally, the business had increased wages in line with the prevailing inflation rate every April, but the recent public successes of 'Newbabes' – winning a small business award and as a result being featured extensively in the national press – had led to a belief amongst the workers that the firm was doing extremely, rather than reasonably, well. They wanted this to be reflected in their pay packets with rises of more than 10 per cent for production line employees.

Steve investigated these key, external and internal factors in a variety of ways – talking to the Department of Trade and Industry and representative bodies about the overseas situation and liaising with various suppliers, respected sales representatives and agents about future supplies of raw materials and component parts from their

▶

present sources. The feedback was that both worries were valid ones, with the outlook decidedly uncertain, and likely to be fraught with problems. Steve chose to switch forth-coming orders to other suppliers who, although they were approximately 10 per cent more expensive, were wholly reliable. He spoke to Raj, head of personnel, who indicated that a wage settlement should be reached shortly with an increase of some 7 per cent to be implemented from April.

With this and other, back up information collected and Mary's sales forecast to hand, Steve began to work on his budget forecast notes. Under 'Materials', he listed all the many items used to make the changing bags and allowed room for volumes, prices and values to be noted – a lengthy list, but essential when each item is an integral part of the finished product and has to be watched carefully. Employees were grouped by jobs with the hours worked, hourly rates of pay and monies due to be paid to them ready to be recorded under volumes, prices and values. Expenditure on equipment and machinery – new items, depreciation on old ones, heat, light, power and the like – was calculated by Cathy who attended to the capital expenditure and administration budget forecasts with proportions then being allocated accordingly to different departments: so Steve just jotted down these main sub-headings at this stage.

So far as the amounts of materials used were concerned, Steve looked at the sales volume figures of Mary's sales budget forecast to estimate the numbers of finished goods required (and when) allowing for the 10 per cent extra as discussed. He then referred to his own production records to calculate the number of raw materials and component parts needed to produce these. Prices (at these levels of usage) could consequently be obtained from suppliers, with allowances made for price rises in due course, and any other external influences. From the estimated, on-going and total production figures, he could then work out the number and type of employees needed at any time, with additional part-timers being brought in as and when necessary. He knew the hourly rates paid, and could liaise with Raj concerning pay rises and other, related matters.

Timings had to be considered carefully, with materials traditionally being brought in the month before usage, and paid for a month afterwards. Ideally, this pattern should continue and, from checking records and discussions with suppliers, Steve saw no reason to suppose otherwise. Wages to staff were paid in the middle of the following month after they were earned – and again this arrangement would carry on throughout the next trading period. Steve could not foresee any external or internal influences that might affect these. Hence, he settled down to switch his figures over to a budget forecast form …

CASE STUDY 2.3   **Composing notes for a capital expenditure budget forecast**

Cathy, co-owner of Newbabes Limited, was responsible for compiling a capital expenditure forecast for the 1998–9 trading period. From discussions with Mary and Steve, she had learned that no new capital items were required to maintain the expected sales and production levels. However, at the same management meeting, Raj of personnel and Adam at distribution indicated that some purchases might be needed elsewhere. The limiting factor so far as Cathy's budget forecast was concerned was that the firm planned to consolidate this year, investigate alternative product and market opportunities and then diversify in the next period. Thus, she did not want to buy any capital items now which might be unsuitable and surplus to requirements later on. Ideally, she did not want to purchase anything!

Cathy began by contemplating the external influences upon her capital expenditure budget forecast and its possible contents – land, buildings, plant, equipment, machinery and vehicles. Despite her considerable reluctance to spend during the period, she knew that she still had to work through each of the potential contents in turn, thinking about their likely relevance and all of the external (and internal) factors that might affect them. Otherwise, something unexpected might arise later on, which could have a huge, negative impact on this and associated budgets. Externally, she was most conscious of a recent visit from a health and safety inspector who had indicated the urgent need to improve and add to toilet and washroom facilities. She had little choice but to go along with this.

With regard to the internal factors influencing her budget, Cathy was particularly concerned about the increased production levels and the corresponding build-up of extra stocks – indeed, Adam's comments at the management meeting had been about the need for more storage space for raw materials, component parts and finished goods. She was also mindful of the antiquated, paper-based information system that existed in the organisation and the need for computerisation, so that documents could be processed more rapidly, invoices issued (and therefore paid) faster and so on. Again, Raj had raised this point in relation to personnel records, and pay. Everyone felt it was an essential step to take, and sooner rather than later.

Like Mary and Steve before her, Cathy believed in keeping budget forecasts as simple as possible – easier said than done with diverse and wide-ranging sales and production forecasts, but achievable with one for capital expenditure, where purchases tended to be fewer and occasional rather than regular. Hence, she just divided her budget forecast into

▶

four sections headed 'toilet and washroom facilities', 'storage facilities', 'computers' and 'miscellaneous items'. This final heading was put in so that any purchases in excess of £500 – and therefore classified as 'capital expenditure' by Newbabes – could be transferred across from their originating budget forecasts into this one in due course.

Calculating the respective volumes required and prices to be paid within each of the headings was a relatively straightforward process. For 'toilet and washroom facilities', she spoke extensively to the health and safety inspector again, planning officers at the local authority, builders, plumbers and electricians. She was particularly mindful throughout of up-and-coming health and safety rules and regulations, so that any building took account of both present and future requirements. Likewise for 'storage facilities', she talked further to builders, after ascertaining from Mary (sales), Steve (production) and Adam (distribution) exactly how much extra room was likely to be needed, where and when. She also took careful note of future needs – especially if the firm diversified – so that any extension would be sufficient for forthcoming growth.

With reference to the 'computers' heading, Cathy discussed the firm's proposed requirements with numerous, prospective suppliers who gave her a clearer idea of the likely costs involved. She was most conscious here of the seemingly endless improvements taking place in computers and wanted to be sure that any system installed would be able to keep pace with developments in this field. Similarly, she talked through any 'miscellaneous' requirements with Mary, Steve, Raj and Adam as and when they produced their own budget forecasts, noting their individual needs for new storage units, or whatever. At all times, Cathy made certain that any planned expenditure complemented not only what the firm would do in the next year, but subsequent to it.

The timing of capital payments was all-important, and needed to take account of the urgency of the purchase, cashflow and possibly, tax considerations too. In terms of urgency, only 'toilet and washroom facilities' could be classified in this way, with prompt expenditure on the others being desirable, rather than essential now. Cashflow was generally good and certainly enough to handle this initial expenditure, with the rest being scheduled as and when required – before storage space ran out, and paperwork overflowed! Having referred to their accountant, Cathy knew that tax implications were not a significant factor on this occasion. Hence, toilet and washroom expenditure was earmarked for the start of the period, storage halfway through and computerisation towards the end – although these could be brought forward if the soon-to-be completed cash budget suggested this was a possibility. Cathy then began transferring her notes onto a budget forecast form.

SUMMARY

1 Substantial preparatory work has to be carried out in order to prepare a budget forecast properly. This involves gathering information, anticipating revenues and estimating expenditure.

2 The information that needs to be accumulated will vary from one situation to another. However, everyone responsible for composing a budget forecast should be aware of:

   (a) any limiting factors that constrain it

   (b) external influences upon it

   (c) internal influences upon it

   (d) any sources of advice that are available

3 When anticipating revenues, it is sensible to make notes about:

   (a) the types of revenue, such as sales and capital injections

   (b) the amounts of revenue, both in terms of quantities and prices

   (c) the timings of revenue, both for sales and capital injections

4 Whilst estimating expenditure, it is wise to produce notes concerning:

   (a) the types of expenditure – start-up, direct, indirect and capital amongst them.

   (b) the amounts of expenditure, with regard to quantities and prices paid

   (c) the timings of expenditure, for start-up, direct, indirect and capital in particular

To compile a budget forecast effectively, you need to concentrate on creating the form for it, accumulating the contents and producing the final version.

CHAPTER THREE

How to compose budget forecasts

- Creating the form
- Accumulating the contents
- Producing the final version
- Summary

Having built up extensive preparatory notes, you should now be in a position to press ahead and actually compile that budget forecast for your department, or whatever. To do this effectively, you need to concentrate on creating the form for it, accumulating the contents and producing the final version – only then can you expect to present your forecast to a budget committee *and* have it approved, hopefully without amendments being made to it.

Creating the form

Some organisations provide standardised budget forecast forms to be completed – most notably for sales, production and capital expenditure as shown in Figures 3.1, 3.2 and 3.3 respectively (see pages 54–9). Others allow their departmental managers or whoever is responsible for filling them in to create their own documents, which may be more appropriate, as circumstances can vary considerably from one department to another.

Whatever your situation is, it is sensible to be aware of the main do's and don'ts of composing or perhaps amending (sometimes quite substantially) a budget forecast form.

Ideally, your form should be:

- basic

- attractive

- compatible.

Basic

Keep the form as simple and as straightforward as you can, so that you are able to complete it comfortably and colleagues can understand it easily. Put in just those major revenue and/or expenditure headings, which need to be included, such as 'direct expenditure' and 'indirect expenditure' in a departmental forecast. Place them in a logical and progressive order.

Do make sure that your form is similar to those drawn up for sales, production, capital expenditure and other departments, as this will stand it in good stead during budget discussions and enable information to be taken from it easily for master budget calculations.

You should consider excluding individual sub-headings like 'rent', 'rates', 'water' and 'heat, light, power', as these may not have to be filled in every time and could therefore either clutter the form unnecessarily and/or be confusing. Leave sufficient room for relevant sub-headings to be added by the person completing the form, where appropriate.

Attractive

You must ensure that your budget forecast form is not only basic but attractive too, so that it helps to present the right image – of a well-thought-out and carefully prepared, professional proposal.

Make certain it is spacious, so that figures can be set apart, and will thus be distinguishable and easy to read. Avoid the use of colour, different or unusual typefaces, highlighted or shaded areas.

These tend to distract or even muddle the reader. Try not to add more than brief explanatory notes, perhaps about how to complete the form (if a colleague is to do it for you), and any key assumptions such as the anticipated rates of interest and inflation that have been (or should be) taken into account. Masses of notes can be offputting.

Compatible

Do make sure that your form is similar to those drawn up for sales, production, capital expenditure and other departments, as this will stand it in good stead during budget discussions and enable information to be taken from it easily for master budget calculations. Choose a standardised layout, typeface and comparable categories, for comparison purposes. An apparently minor point perhaps, but do make sure it is the same size too – A4 or possibly A3 – so that it has a similar 'feel' and status. An A5 form somehow seems less important and can be mislaid readily as well. An example of a departmental budget forecast form is shown as Figure 3.4. An action checklist for creating your own effective form is reproduced as Figure 3.5 (on page 64).

SALES BUDGET FORECAST _____		January			February		
		Est.	Act.	Var.	Est.	Act.	Var.
Category _____ _____	Volume						
	Price						
	Value						
Category _____ _____	Volume						
	Price						
	Value						
Category _____ _____	Volume						
	Price						
	Value						
Category _____ _____	Volume						
	Price						
	Value						
Category _____ _____	Volume						
	Price						
	Value						
Category _____ _____	Volume						
	Price						
	Value						
Category _____ _____	Volume						
	Price						
	Value						
Category _____ _____	Volume						
	Price						
	Value						
Total _____ _____	Volume						
	Price						
	Value						

Category: To be classified by product groups, sales representatives' territories, markets or whatever. An additional sheet will be required if more than eight categories exist, as shown here.

Volume/price/value: 'Volume' and 'value' rows must be completed. You may prefer to compose your form without the 'price' row if this is less appropriate in your circumstances.

Figure 3.1   Sales budget forecast form: an example

March			April			May			June		
Est.	Act.	Var.	Est.	Act.	Var.	Est.	Act.	Var.	Est.	Act.	Var.

Est/act/var: 'Estimated', 'actual' and 'variance'. The second two columns are rather superfluous in a forecast but are included here to emphasise budgeting's control function. Their subsequent inclusion would enable the budget forecast to be monitored, if passed as it stands. It happens sometimes!

The full budget forecast would have a 'Totals' column at the far right after December.

PRODUCTION BUDGET FORECAST _____	January			February		
	Est.	Act.	Var.	Est.	Act.	Var.
Materials						
Total materials (£)						
Labour						
Total labour (£)						
Overheads						
Total overheads (£)						
Grand total (£)						

Materials/labour/overheads: To be completed according to individual circumstances.

Est/act/var: 'Estimated', 'actual', 'variance'. These three columns would allow an accepted budget forecast to be subsequently assessed regularly.

The complete budget forecast form would have a 'Totals' column to the far right after 'December'.

Figure 3.2   Production budget forecast form: an example

March			April			May			June		
Est.	Act.	Var.	Est.	Act.	Var.	Est.	Act.	Var.	Est.	Act.	Var.

CAPITAL EXPENDITURE BUDGET FORECAST _____	January			February		
	Est.	Act.	Var.	Est.	Act.	Var.
Buildings						
Total buildings (£)						
Plant						
Total plant (£)						
Equipment						
Total equipment (£)						
Machinery						
Total machinery (£)						
Vehicles						
Total vehicles (£)						
Grand total (£)						

Buildings/plant/equipment/machinery: To be filled in according to the particular situation.

Est/act/var: 'Estimated', 'actual', 'variance'. Having three columns is useful – they enable an approved budget forecast to be checked on a regular, on-going basis.

The full budget forecast form would include a 'Totals' column to the far right following 'December'.

Figure 3.3   Capital expenditure budget forecast form: an example

March			April			May			June		
Est.	Act.	Var.	Est.	Act.	Var.	Est.	Act.	Var.	Est.	Act.	Var.

Accumulating the contents

With the form drawn up, it is sensible to photocopy it, so that you can then study and pencil in your numerous revenue and expenditure figures:

- down the side
- across the top
- in the middle.

Down the side

Whether you are completing a sales, production, capital expenditure or departmental budget forecast, you should initially fill in the left side of the form. Ideally, this will provide the main headings for guidance (if necessary), but be flexible enough to allow you to insert the sub-headings that are most applicable to your situation. In a sales budget, you will list your products and/or services *or* sales representatives by name or territory *or* individual markets, according to your particular circumstances. You may have to move on to a second sheet, depending on the number of categories involved.

Similarly, you may include named sub-headings for the material, labour and overhead costs of the production budget, buildings, plant, equipment, machinery and vehicles for the capital expenditure budget plus start-up, direct, indirect and capital costs for the departmental budget. As with the sales budget form which has ready-made volume, price and value lines, it is helpful if you can write these into your budget too. They will make it easier for you to monitor the budget more closely and accurately later on, when you want to spot variances in terms of quantities sold or purchased and prices charged or paid for. Again, a follow-up sheet might be required, depending on how much you have to put into the form.

Across the top

Not surprisingly, the top of your sales, production, capital expenditure or departmental budget form is almost certainly the simplest part that you will have to fill out. You just need to state the period it covers (2000 or 2000/1, as examples), followed by the sub-periods; January 2000, February 2000 and so on, or whatever. Your company may budget over 12 monthly sub-periods or 13 four-weekly sub-periods. Both are equally appropriate, so long as everyone knows what is happening and is co-ordinated, and data can be recorded and is available at the correct times.

In the middle

Regardless of the type of budget form you are responsible for dealing with, it will hopefully be divided up into three columns – for estimated figures to be put in now and actual and variance figures to be placed there at a later date, as and when they become known to you. For the sales budget forecast, you will have to refer back to your collected notes, subsequently recording the anticipated amounts, prices and timings of each product group's, sales representative's or market's revenues in the estimated columns for January, February and so forth.

Much the same process has to be carried out if you are working on an expenditure-orientated budget forecast – checking notes and then detailing the amounts, prices and timings of material, labour and overhead costs in a production budget forecast, buildings, plant and the like for capital expenditure and start-up, direct costs and so on for a departmental one. Although you will normally be expected to explain and talk through the figures at the upcoming budget committee meeting, you may wish to add one or two explanations here and there. If so, put (1), (2) and so forth next to the appropriate sub-headings, with the reference numbers and brief commentaries at the bottom of the sheet, or overleaf. Case study 3.1 is an example of this.

———— BUDGET FORECAST ————	January			February		
	Est.	Act.	Var.	Est.	Act.	Var.
Start-up						
Total start-up (£)						
Direct						
Total direct (£)						
Indirect						
Total indirect (£)						
Capital						
Total capital (£)						
Grand total (£)						

Start up/direct/indirect/capital: To be completed in line with the specific circumstances.

Figure 3.4   Departmental budget forecast form: an example

March			April			May			June		
Est.	Act.	Var.	Est.	Act.	Var.	Est.	Act.	Var.	Est.	Act.	Var.

Est/act/var: 'Estimated', 'actual', 'variance'. Including these three columns means a successful budget forecast can consequently be monitored properly.

The complete budget forecast would have a 'Totals' column to the far right, following 'December'.

If you have created an effective form, you will be able to say 'yes' to all of these questions. Any 'no's, and there is room for improvements to be made!

	Yes	No		Yes	No
Are just the essential revenue and expenditure headings included?	☐	☐	Have you kept any explanatory notes brief and to the point?	☐	☐
Have you put them in a logical and progressive order?	☐	☐	Is the form an attractive one?	☐	☐
Have individual sub-headings been excluded?	☐	☐	Does it convey a well prepared, professional image?	☐	☐
Have you left sufficient room for relevant sub-headings to be added?	☐	☐	Have you chosen a standardised layout and typeface?	☐	☐
Is the form a simple and straightforward one?	☐	☐	Do your categories match those used in other forms?	☐	☐
Can you complete it comfortably?	☐	☐	Is your form the same size as others?	☐	☐
Will your colleagues be able to understand it easily?	☐	☐	Is this form compatible with others in the company?	☐	☐
Is the form spacious and roomy?	☐	☐	Can it be referred to easily during master budget calculations?	☐	☐
Have you avoided the use of colour, different and unusual typefaces, highlighted and shaded areas?	☐	☐	In short, is this an effective form?	☐	☐

Figure 3.5   Creating your own form: an action checklist

CASE STUDY 3.1   **Pencilling in a departmental budget forecast form**

Adam was the distribution manager at Newbabes Limited, and his work included taking finished goods from the factory, storing them properly, watching stock levels, reporting potential shortages and excessive reserves to Steve, receiving sales orders from Mary, liaising with Cathy about payment and credit positions, packing and posting goods, dealing with returns and corresponding paperwork. He also had to draw up a distribution budget forecast for 1998–9 which he approached in the same way that Mary, Steve and Cathy did earlier. An extract from Adam's sketched out figures – ready to be transferred to a form – are as shown below:

		April	May	June	July
(1)	Staff wages	2,300	2,500	2,500	2,500
(2)	Stationery	400	400	400	600
(3)	Packaging	600	700	600	700
(4)	Postage	600	700	600	700
(5)	Independent carrier	150	150	150	150
(6)	Miscellaneous items	250	250	250	250
(7)	**Total**	**4,300**	**4,700**	**4,500**	**4,900**

Although the five managers within Newbabes were expected to present and discuss their budget forecasts at a forthcoming, weekly management meeting, Adam felt it would be advisable to circulate copies of his forecast to his colleagues in advance of that meeting, in order that they could take account of it, if relevant, in their calculations. Adam knew the figures, the reasons and the workings behind them absolutely inside out but realised that these would not be so apparent to the others. Thus, he added brief, explanatory notes at the bottom of the form, some of which are reproduced here:

(1) **Staff wages.** Distribution manager's at £1,500 per month to April, £1,605 thereafter. Three part-timers working three, three and four hours each day respectively at £4 per hour to April and at £4.40 after that.
(200 hours per month at £4 = £800; 200 hours at £4.40 = £880.)

(2) **Stationery.** Approximately 5,300 units processed by the department each month, and averaging three documents for completion per process at £25 for 1,000 documents = £400 per month. An allowance has been made for purchasing computer stationery in July to coincide with the planned computerisation of the firm at that time.

Producing the final version

Once you have pencilled the various revenue and/or expenditure figures on to a photo-copied budget forecast form, you can set about the original's appearance and contents, getting it ready to be presented to a budget committee. Your filled-in form needs to be:

- complete

- clear

- accurate.

Complete

Obviously, your budget forecast does need to be completed fully, supplying *all* of the information that is likely to be required by the budget committee. If you are using a standardised form with one or two columns or rows which do not have to be filled out by you, put dashes in to indicate this rather than leaving them blank, as other readers will not know if these spaces are there by oversight or intention. Ideally, your form should be detailed enough to stand alone, and be presented without further explanation or additional questions needing to be asked and answered.

> It is a good idea to show your form to a colleague prior to submission, to ensure that he or she thinks it is as understandable as you do – often he or she will not!

Clear

To be presentable, the budget forecast must also be clear and simple to understand. More often than not, this just means paying attention to relatively minor details – making sure that figures are well-separated, commas and decimal points are in the right places, supporting text is readable with grammar, spelling and punctuation all correct and short words and phrases are used instead of slang, jargon, technical or vague expressions. It is a good idea to show your form to a colleague prior to submission, to ensure that he or she thinks it is as understandable as you do – often he or she will not!

Accurate

You do need to ensure that your budget forecast is scrupulously accurate – an obvious point perhaps, but one which often seems to be overlooked, with potentially disastrous consequences. Again, this really involves little more than being attentive and checking back over what you have put down – making certain that information has been placed in the right columns and rows, figures have been added up and subtracted properly and totals are all correct. Never forget you are dealing with dozens – if not hundreds – of figures; one slip here or there can affect everything else. A completed departmental budget forecast form is shown as Figure 3.6 and an action checklist is shown in Figure 3.7 (on page 70).

PERSONNEL BUDGET FORECAST _____	January			February		
	Est.	Act.	Var.	Est.	Act.	Var.
Start-up						
Consultancy services (Grimm and Bradshaw)	5,000			—		
Consultancy services (Hopkins Partnership)	—			10,000		
Total start-up (£)	**5,000**			**10,000**		
Direct						
Skilled labour	100,000			100,000		
Semi-skilled labour	50,000			50,000		
Unskilled labour	55,000			55,000		
Total direct (£)	**205,000**			**205,000**		
Indirect						
Senior management	16,000			16,000		
Middle management	20,000			20,000		
Junior management	20,000			20,000		
Total indirect (£)	**56,000**			**56,000**		
Capital						
——N/A——	—			—		
Total capital (£)	**—**			**—**		
Grand total (£)	**266,000**			**266,000**		

Start up/direct/indirect/capital: Filled in as appropriate for this personnel department. Ideally, each sub-heading – 'skilled labour', 'semi-skilled labour' and so on – would have been analysed further in terms of volume, price and value. It may be assumed for this example that the departmental manager would discuss these details at the forthcoming budget committee meeting.

Figure 3.6   Completed departmental budget forecast form: an example

March			April			May			June		
Est.	Act.	Var.	Est.	Act.	Var.	Est.	Act.	Var.	Est.	Act.	Var.
—			—			—			—		
—			—			—			—		
—			—			—			—		
—			—			—			—		
100,000			100,000			100,000			100,000		
50,000			50,000			50,000			50,000		
55,000			55,000			55,000			55,000		
205,000			205,000			205,000			205,000		
16,000			16,000			16,000			16,000		
20,000			20,000			20,000			20,000		
20,000			20,000			20,000			20,000		
56,000			56,000			56,000			56,000		
—			—			—			—		
—			—			—			—		
261,000			261,000			261,000			261,000		

You should be able to answer the following questions positively, assuming that you have filled in your form properly. If you cannot, have another go!

	Yes	No
Has the form been completed fully?	☐	☐
Have you filled in every space; with a dash if necessary?	☐	☐
Is the form detailed enough to stand alone?	☐	☐
Does it provide sufficient explanation?	☐	☐
Does it answer all probable questions?	☐	☐
Does it supply all of the information likely to be required by the budget committee?	☐	☐
Are the contents clear and easy to understand?	☐	☐
Are the figures separated out?	☐	☐
Have you put commas and decimal points in the right places?	☐	☐

	Yes	No
Is the text readable?	☐	☐
Are grammar, spelling and punctuation all correct?	☐	☐
Have you used short words and phrases?	☐	☐
Have you avoided slang, jargon, technical and vague expressions?	☐	☐
Has a colleague studied the form, and agreed it is understandable?	☐	☐
Is the form absolutely accurate?	☐	☐
Have you put information in the right columns and rows?	☐	☐
Have you added, subtracted and totalled figures properly?	☐	☐
In brief, is this a well completed form?	☐	☐

Figure 3.7   Completing a form successfully: an action checklist

SUMMARY

1 Some businesses provide standardised budget forecast forms for completion. Those that need to be created for individual, specific circumstances must be:

(a) basic

(b) attractive

(c) compatible with others

2 It is sensible to pencil in a photocopy of the form, putting full and detailed figures carefully:

(a) down the side

(b) across the top

(c) in the middle

3 A final version of the budget forecast form can then be produced and polished. To be presented to a budget committee, it has to be:

(a) complete

(b) clear

(c) accurate

To put forward your budget forecast, you need to know about the budget committee, the budget meeting and how a master budget is set.

CHAPTER FOUR

What you need to know about submitting budget forecasts

- The role of a budget committee

- Participating successfully in committee meetings

- Developing the master budget

- Summary

You should now be ready and able to put forward your sales, production, capital expenditure or departmental budget forecast to a budget committee – and hopefully, have it approved as it stands, or with little more than minor amendments being made to it. With regard to this stage of the budgetary process, you need to know something about the role of a budget committee, how to participate successfully at a committee meeting, *and* how a master budget is developed, and set.

The role of a budget committee

In most organisations, a budget committee plays a central role in the initiation, formulation and maintenance of budgets. As you will almost certainly be expected to participate in budget committee meetings at this point in the proceedings, you ought to be broadly familiar with the committee's likely:

- make up
- activities.

Make-up

Inevitably, the make-up of a budget committee will depend mainly upon the size, type and nature of the organisation in question. It has been stated that in a larger, multi-layered concern, an effective budget committee will comprise of members drawn from three key groups. Executive management will be represented in order to provide a broad, corporate overview, ensure budgets fit into the company's objectives and to make (or at least rubber-stamp) the final decisions. Senior 'budget holders' – those people responsible for overseeing major functional and/or departmental budgets – will be present to participate in discussions, and perhaps budget setting procedures. The accounting function – typically in the guise of the chief accountant or financial controller – will be on hand to supply specialist advice and assistance.

In some, bigger companies, a 'budget officer' (or manager) will be employed, working alongside, or answering to, the finance director, chief accountant or financial controller. His or her duties might include initiating the budgetary process, liaising with and advising departmental and section heads, convening and perhaps chairing budget committee meetings and supervising monitoring, remedial and review activities thereafter, once budgets have been finalised. As an alternative to employing a specialist budget officer, other firms will simply incorporate these tasks and responsibilities within the chief accountant's remit.

Activities

Most – if not all – non-financial managers within a company will assume that a budget committee exists purely to approve and/or amend budget forecasts, and to create a master budget. It is fair to state that this is its predominant role in the majority of organisations. Nonetheless, within this rather broad all-encompassing activity, numerous other tasks can be readily identified, all of which are of some significance to the overall planning and control function.

A budget committee may set the budget period and consequently, the length of all the budgets to be drawn up. Although most budgets will be composed for a one-year period – usually coinciding with the calendar or firm's accounting year – they can cover a shorter or longer timescale. Much depends on the type and nature of the particular business and – most significantly – the trade or industry within which it is operating. Trading in rapidly changing conditions indicates the need for much shorter, closely controlled budgets; more stable, slow-to-change circumstances enable lengthier budgets to be scheduled.

Equally, sub-periods will be set by the budget committee too. Ideally, these will be established individually for the various budgets, and according to how closely each one needs to be monitored; again, a volatile, ever-changing scenario implies much closer control is required, whilst a steadier environment signifies the need for less frequent monitoring. As examples, a sales budget may have to be looked at on a weekly or monthly basis, whilst administration might be reviewed quarterly. Of course, much will depend on the availability of data – support systems must exist to enable them to be produced at the appropriate times.

A budget committee could also specify the revenue and expenditure categories to be adopted on a company-wide basis – perhaps 'start-up', 'direct', 'indirect' and 'capital expenditure'. Obviously, the exact types, number and names of these categories will vary from one firm to another. For example, a business which is not planning to diversify in the foreseeable future is unlikely to incur any start-up costs whilst another might prefer to divide direct costs into more than one category – 'cost of materials' and 'wages', perhaps. These categories must be understood by everyone throughout the company, and applied consistently, so that consequently details can be transferred accurately to the master budget.

Similarly, sub-categories will often be determined by the budget committee too – indeed, some organisations dispense with the overall category headings altogether and simply draw up a lengthier list of what would otherwise be described as sub-categories – rent, rates, water and so on. Typically, these will be based on the numerous entries within the firm's books, ledgers and end of year accounts. Hopefully, they will be broad enough to plan and control properly, but not so detailed that monitoring becomes time-consuming and difficult. As an example, 'stationery' should suffice for 'rubbers', 'pens', 'paper clips' and so forth. Again, everybody in the organisation should be aware of and familiar with these, so that they can be applied in a uniform manner.

General guidelines for compiling, submitting and monitoring budgets will be issued by the budget committee. These will usually comprise fairly straightforward instructions – such as 'complete all lines and columns, putting "n/a" where appropriate' – designed to ensure budgets are prepared and controlled along comparable lines. Budget assumptions – like 'inflation is expected to rise by 3 per cent during the period' and 'exchange rates are to remain the same' – will also be devised, and everyone is expected to allow for and abide by these. Some larger concerns will incorporate these details – and other miscellaneous facts and figures such as classification codes for revenue and expenditure items – into a budget manual. Extracts from such a manual are reproduced as Figures 4.1 and 4.2.

- Draw a black line through those headings and sections which do not apply to you.

- Complete all remaining sections, putting 'n/a' or a dash where appropriate, rather than leaving any boxes blank.

- Include sub-headings which suit your requirements, taking these from sales and bought ledger entry headings.

- Use black ink when noting figures.

- Double-check all figures after completion, especially the totals.

- Keep any explanatory notes to a minimum.

- Write supporting text in block capitals, or type, preferably.

- Avoid highlighting, underlining or in any way emphasising the text.

- If you are not sure how to complete your budget forecast, or have any other queries contact your line manager immediately.

Figure 4.1   Budget manual: an extract (general guidelines)

Often, non-financial managers' only real contact and involvement with a budget committee will be at the annual meeting (or whenever), where they are expected to present and discuss their budget forecast, as appropriate (although in practice it can involve several meetings to allow for discussions, amendments, resubmissions and final agreement). The committee tries at this time to ensure that all budgets conform to the company's objectives, are reasonable and attainable (having taken account of all possible internal and external influences) and budgets and budget holders are co-ordinated so that they act in unison rather than separately.

When composing your budget forecast for the forthcoming period, the following assumptions should be taken into account:

- **Prices.** We expect to increase the selling prices of all our goods by 5 per cent from January.

- **Market conditions.** We predict a 6 per cent rise in consumer spending with us in comparison with the preceding period and sub-periods.

- **Debtors.** We anticipate that 80 per cent of payments due to us will be made within 30 days of receipt of invoice, with the remaining 20 per cent within 60 days.

- **Suppliers (raw materials/component parts).** An across the board, 5 per cent increase in purchase prices should be assumed from January.

- **Inflation.** A steady inflation rate of 3 per cent is anticipated for the period.

- **Exchange rates.** Assume that exchange rates will remain the same throughout the period.

- **Creditors.** All invoices will be settled by us within 30 days of their receipt.

- **Taxation.** Assume that value-added tax rates will stay unchanged during the period.

- **Interest rates.** We estimate that base, overdraft and loan rates will remain at the same levels for the whole period.

- **Wages.** We anticipate an across the board, 3 per cent rise in wage payments, commencing in April. The costs of statutory obligations are expected to stay unchanged.

Individual assumptions for revenues and expenditure specific only to your budget should be made by you and discussed with the budget committee in accordance with previously agreed, set procedures.

Figure 4.2   Budget manual: another extract (budget assumptions)

Here is a list of some of the key 'what if?' questions that may be raised at a budget committee meeting. You need to decide which ones could affect your budget and, if appropriate, in what ways. You might be able to think of other questions that are relevant to your particular situation too, subsequently calculating their likely consequences as well.

What if ...	Relevant	Irrelevant	What if ...	Relevant	Irrelevant
Sales rise or fall more than anticipated?	☐	☐	Administrative costs move upwards or downwards?	☐	☐
Are paid for earlier or later than expected?	☐	☐	Are settled earlier or later on?	☐	☐
Production costs go up or down?	☐	☐	Personnel costs differ, either favourably or unfavourably?	☐	☐
Are settled more quickly or slowly?	☐	☐	Are paid more quickly or more slowly than suggested?	☐	☐
Purchasing costs increase or decrease?	☐	☐	Other costs rise, fall or are settled sooner or later than envisaged?	☐	☐
Are paid for sooner or later than planned?	☐	☐	Inflation rates improve or worsen?	☐	☐
Marketing costs vary upwards or downwards?	☐	☐	Interest rates are raised or lowered?	☐	☐
Are settled more quickly or more slowly than estimated?	☐	☐	Taxation threshold and rates change?	☐	☐
Finance costs are more or less than predicted?	☐	☐	Tariffs are increased or decreased?	☐	☐
Are paid for in advance of or after the planned dates?	☐	☐	Quotas are imposed, adjusted or removed?	☐	☐
			General circumstances		

Figure 4.3   'What if?' questions: a checklist

Much of the committee's work at this stage will involve raising numerous 'what if?' questions, calculating the probabilities of certain hypothetical situations developing and evaluating the possible consequences of those that do. As examples: what if sales volumes fall by 5 per cent? What if distribution costs rise by 10 per cent? What if exchange rates fluctuate by 10 per cent in our favour? Or even 15 per cent, perhaps? The other way? Ideally, such questions will have been addressed by a budget holder, before the relevant budget forecast is put forward – even if it needs to be done at the last moment. A list of 'what if?' questions is shown as Figure 4.3.

Having reached a consensus about the submitted budget forecasts, the budget committee – or more likely those members of it who represent the accounting function – may amalgamate all of them into a single, composite budget. This depends mainly upon the size of the concern, how it is structured, and how far owners and/or directors are willing to delegate the planning and control functions. Typically, smaller concerns tend to create one, company-wide budget whereas larger businesses plan and control by using numerous, separate budgets, effectively operating with some degree of independence from each other. An example of a composite budget is reproduced as Figure 4.4 (see pages 82–3).

> Much of the committee's work at this stage will involve raising numerous 'what if?' questions, calculating the probabilities of certain hypothetical situations developing and evaluating the possible consequences of those that do.

Whatever the size and type of firm, the budget committee – or at least its key, financial members – will draw up a budgeted profit and loss account, cash budget and a budgeted balance sheet, all derived from the single or numerous budgets in existence. In practice, this stage of the proceedings will involve further discussions in or out of committee meeting, as combining budget forecasts and their data can highlight problems which would arise if those forecasts were ratified as budgets. For example, the early purchase of capital equipment could create cashflow difficulties for the entire firm later on. Hence some budget forecasts will be adjusted so that they all fit together well.

Thereafter, the budget committee's (or the budget officer's) work will mainly be in an overall, supervisory capacity. Departmental or sectional teams will probably monitor revenues and expenditure and review progress of the budgets at regular intervals, reporting variances and prospective problems to the appropriate budget holders. They will then initiate whatever actions are necessary to eliminate future variances and avoid forthcoming problems. Those difficulties that cannot be dealt with in the department or section – raw material costs are spiralling out of control, production equipment has broken down irretrievably – will be referred upwards to the committee.

> Whatever the size and type of firm, the budget committee – or at least its key, financial members – will draw up a budgeted profit and loss account, cash budget and a budgeted balance sheet, all derived from the single or numerous budgets in existence.

The budget committee (or the budget officer) will advise accordingly, calling a meeting as and when necessary to notify all of its members. If the difficulty cannot be resolved, all (or just the affected) budgets will be amended for the duration of the period. The committee's activities then effectively begin again on a cyclical basis, with the next budget period and sub-periods, categories and sub-categories being established. A worked through example of the role of a budget committee is explained further in Case study 4.1.

CASE STUDY 4.1   Role of a budget committee

In 'Newbabes', the budget committee was structured in a very loose and flexible manner, as often happens in smaller organisations. Cathy – co-owner and responsible for compiling capital expenditure, finance and administration budget forecasts – headed the formal meeting at which Mary, Steve, Raj and Adam presented and subsequently discussed their forecasts for the coming period. In essence, Mary, Steve, Raj and Adam took the roles of senior budget holders. Given her activities before, during and after the meeting, Cathy could be described as chief executive, financial controller *and* budget officer, all rolled into one!

Similarly, the budget committee's activities were conducted informally too. The budget period established itself automatically on the commencement of the business and had continued to run parallel with the trading year ever since. Sub-periods seemed to divide themselves naturally on a monthly basis – although each of the managers did monitor developments day-by-day and week-by-week, as necessary. Categories and sub-categories of revenue and expenditure were chosen by the appropriate managers with references being made to each other (and particularly Cathy) in times of doubt. Unwritten guidelines and assumptions developed as a result of comments made during weekly management meetings – 'I think it would be a good idea if we did this from now on', 'I see such-and-such is expected to happen next year', and so forth.

At the main budget committee meeting itself, each manager took it in turns to present their budget forecast. As every forecast had been built up in close liaison with the other managers *and* had been circulated prior to the meeting, this enabled the remaining managers to play devil's advocate. They did it well, seeking continually to find flaws in the figures and reasoning behind them. It was a tough process – but most forecasts and figures remained wholly intact. Thereafter, Cathy took all the forecasts and notes of any suggested amendments arising from the meeting and produced the master budget documents from them. This was a fairly intricate process and Cathy's conclusions – and any changes needed to produce an acceptable overall result – were invariably taken without comment, or further discussion.

After that, Cathy, Mary, Steve, Raj and Adam took charge of their own budgets (albeit with Cathy acting simultaneously in a co-ordinating and advisory role). Assistants were expected to record and file documents properly *and* promptly, referring key data up to their manager each month or as and when problems arose. Each manager had to fill in the relevant section of their budget every month, reporting progress (and any difficulties) at the next management meeting. Minor concerns were left to the individual manager to deal with whilst more serious ones were subjected to discussion and (hopefully) universal agreement about how to approach them. Newbabes was always quick to adjust its budgets and master budgets in the light of irreversible developments – often, three or four times a year.

ABM LTD BUDGET 1999	January			February		
	Est.	Act.	Var.	Est.	Act.	Var.
Revenues:						
Sales (north)	20,000			23,000		
Sales (east)	18,000			18,000		
Sales (central)	22,000			25,000		
Sales (west)	14,000			14,000		
Sales (south)	18,000			18,000		
Other	—			—		
Total revenues (£)	**92,000**			**98,000**		
Expenditure:						
Production	31,000			33,000		
Marketing	20,000			22,000		
Finance	5,000			5,000		
Administration	6,000			6,000		
Personnel	20,000			20,000		
Distribution	8,000			8,000		
Capital	—			—		
Total expenditure (£)	**90,000**			**94,000**		
Profit (£)	**2,000**			**4,000**		

Figure 4.4   Composite budget: an example

March			April			May			June		
Est.	Act.	Var.	Est.	Act.	Var.	Est.	Act.	Var.	Est.	Act.	Var.
23,000			28,000			28,000			28,000		
19,000			19,000			19,000			18,000		
28,000			28,000			28,000			26,000		
15,000			16,000			18,000			16,000		
18,000			20,000			20,000			22,000		
—			25,000			—			—		
103,000			**136,000**			**113,000**			**110,000**		
35,000			37,000			38,000			37,000		
25,000			22,000			22,000			22,000		
5,000			5,000			5,000			5,000		
6,000			6,000			6,000			6,000		
26,000			20,000			20,000			26,000		
8,000			8,000			8,000			8,000		
—			—			25,000			—		
105,000			**98,000**			**124,000**			**104,000**		
(2,000)			**38,000**			**(11,000)**			**6,000**		

Participating successfully in committee meetings

With a clearer idea of the workings of the budget committee you are due to face, it is sensible to consider how you should approach the meeting so that your budget forecast is accepted in its entirety, or with minimal changes being made to it.

View your participation in three stages:

- before the committee meeting
- during the committee meeting
- after the committee meeting.

Before the committee meeting

Preparation is the key to attending a budget committee meeting successfully – and this means putting in as much work as possible beforehand. To start with, find out everything there is to know about the meeting itself – its date, start and finish times, duration, location, purpose, topics and participants. This and other relevant data should be available from the agenda which is usually circulated a week or so before the event. If one is not supplied, approach the budget officer, chief accountant or whoever is arranging and/or chairing the meeting, in order to ascertain these facts.

Next, you must contemplate in some detail the other people who will take part in the committee meeting – senior executives, fellow budget holders and the chief accountant, for example. Consider their aims and topics of interest, and how these match or differ from your own. You may find it helpful to work out who has the most influence at this meeting and who may or may not support you, so that their assistance can be enlisted in advance and/or likely comments and objections identified in order that responses can be prepared for them.

Study the topics to be discussed in turn – sales budget forecast, production budget forecast, departmental ones and so on. Think again how each of these can affect your own budget, for better or for worse. To be fully prepared, it may be appropriate in some instances to try to obtain relevant budget forecasts to double-check that you have taken account of them, and that your one fits into the overall picture planned by the budget committee.

Then, you must plan what *you* are expected to do in the committee meeting – most likely, presenting your budget forecast, discussing and answering questions about it at some stage, listening to other members speak and asking them questions about their proposals for the remainder of the time. Concentrating on your speech to begin with, you need to think about why you are speaking, what you are seeking to achieve, who your audience is, what they want to know, how long you are due to talk for, and how it fits into the agenda.

From your answers to these self-directed questions, you can go on to prepare a speech, sketching out a framework of points to talk through; perhaps the various revenue and expenditure categories and sub-categories, amounts and timings of each in sequence.

You may wish to jot down numerous key words and phrases, anticipated responses to comments, suggestions and objections on a postcard for easy reference, and provide details of your budget forecast in pre-circulated handouts and/or on a flip chart or overhead projector transparency at the committee meeting itself.

It is sensible to rehearse what you are going to say – out loud in front of a mirror, camcorder or, preferably, respected colleagues who know about budgets, can speak well themselves and are able to criticise you constructively. Should you be working with handouts, a flip chart or an overhead projector, then incorporate these in your rehearsals too. Ask respected colleagues to raise probable 'what if?' questions, so that you can run through your prepared responses.

Try not to over-rehearse though – if you do and it all goes according to plan on the day, your speech will still sound stilted, rather than spontaneous. If something unexpected happens, you might be thrown completely and find yourself lost for words.

Whether you assess yourself by playing back a video of your speech or ask others to appraise it, you need to focus on four, main areas – contents, style, equipment and length.

Regarding contents, did you include everything? Is it a good framework, well-structured and in a logical order, making it easy to move from one point to another? Concerning your style, were you brisk and businesslike? Did you use clear and concise words, phrases and sentences? Provide succinct explanations and answers to questions? Any mistakes and shortcomings must be identified and changes made *now* during your rehearsal rather than at the meeting itself.

If equipment such as a flipchart or an overhead projector is being used, you need to evaluate how well you are handling them at the moment. Did they fit in successfully at rehearsal? Can you switch easily from speaking to showing and back again, as relevant? Avoid making any mistakes? Did any mishaps occur? The length of the speech must be considered too – no doubt you will be expected to talk for perhaps five minutes or whatever, but no longer. Did you finish on time? Too short? Perhaps you omitted a key point or needed to add more details to others. Too long? Maybe you were rambling a little, or repeating explanations. Again, changes have to be made immediately.

Make sure everyone around you knows that you are attending a budget committee meeting, informing them of the date, time, place and duration well in advance. Insist you are not interrupted during that time.

Before going in, switch off mobile phones, bleepers and the like. Do not be delayed by last minute conversations, phone calls or tasks – if you are late, it will not only create the impression that you are rude and/or disorganised, but could result in key information being missed, that might affect you.

Take in the main documents – notes, handouts of your budget forecast, overhead projector transparencies, a notepad, pen and pencil.

During the committee meeting

Most budget committee meetings will follow a similar sequence of activities. Typically a meeting will start with the chairperson – whether the chief executive, chief accountant or budget officer – outlining the purpose of the meeting, and the topics to be discussed. A speech may then be made by a senior executive, perhaps detailing the company's past performance, current objectives and future plans, thus putting budgeting into its overall context within the firm. Presentations of the various budget forecasts will be made by the appropriate budget holders and discussed as relevant. The chairperson will then conclude the meeting by summarising what has happened, and indicating that the master budget will be drafted shortly thereafter.

Thus, you need to approach the budget committee meeting that you are attending both as a speaker – albeit perhaps only for a few, brief minutes – *and* as a participant listening to others for the rest of the time.

As a speaker, you should have planned, prepared and rehearsed what you are going to say so that its contents, style and length are all satisfactory. You now need to concentrate more fully on actually making that speech in the most effective manner and using that equipment successfully.

With this in mind, you must contemplate initially your appearance as you address your fellow committee members.

Smart dress – collar and tie and the like – is usually a wise choice, as this acknowledges the importance of the meeting and signifies respect for the other people present. However, your appearance does depend largely upon what is considered acceptable within your own organisation.

From a speaking viewpoint, it is essential that you are comfortable with what you are wearing. An itchy new shirt or blouse, thick and heavy jacket, tight trousers or skirt and pinched shoes will feel unpleasant, and distract you from your work.

Often, *how* you say something is as relevant as *what* you say, particularly if you want colleagues to listen carefully and (hopefully) agree with you.

Make certain you are heard by holding up your head, opening your mouth wide and speaking out in a clear, strong voice. Vary it to maintain interest – especially important when you are relaying facts and figures – by speaking slightly faster to convey urgency and more slowly to emphasise certain points. A higher pitch indicates enthusiasm, whilst a lower one further helps to stress the major points being made. Pause for effect as and when you want colleagues to reflect on a specific comment.

Similarly, how you look when you are talking is of some significance – if *you* appear bored when putting across details of anticipated revenues, then other people in the room are likely to feel the same way too, and will switch off mentally. Your facial expressions should match what you are saying, in order to support the points you are making – sincere, serious, enthusiastic about a possible capital expenditure project, and so on. Maintain eye contact with colleagues as well – to attract and hold their attention, build support and obtain feedback. Do not simply concentrate on the chairperson or whoever has most influence on the decision-making process; look regularly and often at everyone, seeking universal approval.

You must think about your body language, to ensure that this backs up rather than detracts from your message, and the various points being made.

Sitting down to speak is informal, friendly and encourages participation and discussion. It is most suited to smaller groups. Standing up creates a more impressive image, shows respect and makes it easier to be heard. This could be a wiser choice if addressing a larger group of people.

Try to keep relatively still as you speak to convey a calm, businesslike manner, although occasional, planned movements such as the sweep of an arm can be effective. Avoid repetitive and annoying mannerisms such as tapping your feet and excessive movements, like waving arms or striding about, which are offputting.

Your speech will probably be supported by visual aids and accompanying equipment – handouts, a flipchart or transparencies on an overhead projector, typically detailing your overall budget forecast, perhaps with explanatory notes. Obviously, these can be advantageous – they help to put over in-depth information quicker and better, add variety to the presentation and enable participants to retain details afterwards for reference purposes. Nevertheless, they do take time and effort to arrange and prepare and can be tricky to handle properly. Sometimes, they can dominate proceedings and distract from your commentary.

If including handouts, use A4 paper rather than A5 sheets so that forms, figures and explanatory text are easy to read. Check for mistakes and errors beforehand, as these would reflect badly on your professionalism and could cause confusion too.

Rewrite or retype as necessary, and photocopy sheets again. Staple pages together so they are less likely to be mislaid by participants. Number the pages anyway – just in case! Circulate handouts before or on arrival at the meeting so that there is enough time to study them before or as you speak. Have spare copies to hand for those participants who forget to bring them along, or need extra ones for absent colleagues.

Use a flipchart *only* if it is visible to everyone in the room. Before you speak, make sure the stand is steady and will not fall over unexpectedly, score pages to be torn off as and when appropriate, which saves a struggle later on, and pencil in headings and sub-headings too, to act as reminders. Have spare paper and marker pens to hand.

When using the flipchart, write in large letters and numbers and avoid writing and talking at the same time, which is always a recipe for disaster! Show each page for at least one minute, giving participants time to note its contents.

Tear off pages as and when you move on, but not before the audience has finished making notes – an obvious point perhaps, but one which many speakers seem to ignore!

If incorporating an overhead projector in your presentation, ensure the projected transparency can be seen by making it as large as possible, and cleaning the surface of the lens of the projector beforehand. Use pre-prepared and numbered transparencies and make certain you know how to put them on the right way up *and* round, and can operate the projector competently – sometimes easier said than done! Dim the lights and/or close the curtains as required, and stand back from the projected image as you speak. Give participants sufficient time to read the data, allowing them to note it down. Don't talk as they read, or repeat what they can see for themselves. Turn off the projector when they have finished and you are ready to go on.

Of course, for most of the budget committee meeting – perhaps 50 or 55 out of 60 minutes – you will be a participant, expected to listen to your colleagues, and contribute only as and when appropriate. As a participant, it is important that you listen carefully so you obtain any information that is relevant to your budget.

You should also be seen to be listening – by looking at the speaker, smiling and nodding encouragement, as this will win approval and make it more likely that they will listen to you when it is your turn to talk.

Avoid staring into space, fidgeting, slouching or being distracted in any way.

Make notes – perhaps adding explanatory comments to a pre-circulated handout about forthcoming sales and production levels – as and when required. This is especially relevant if you are receiving new or revised information which may be of significance to your budget forecast, which you could be expected to amend after the meeting. Ask questions when necessary to verify facts. Do this after the person has finished speaking, signalling for attention and directing your query through the chairperson, as a matter of courtesy. Steer clear of interrupting anyone or holding breakaway discussions.

As a general rule, you should ask questions or make points only if you have something valuable to contribute – to seek clarification of an unclear statement made by a speaker, to provide an explanation of how your activities or budget may affect others, and so on. It should not be seen as an opportunity to score political points, embarrass or put down a colleague in any way. The committee meeting should be regarded as a *team* effort, designed to co-ordinate everyone and everything together, *not* as a divisive free-for-all.

After the committee meeting

The majority of budget committee meetings will end with one or more budget holders being asked to revise their budget forecasts in the light of additional information having been raised during the various speeches and discussions. Perhaps the purchasing manager has highlighted likely delays in obtaining sufficient quantities of raw materials at certain times which will have a knock-on effect on production and sales, at least.

As a general rule, you should ask questions or make points only if you have something valuable to contribute – to seek clarification of an unclear statement made by a speaker, to provide an explanation of how your activities or budget may affect others, and so on.

Possibly, the urgent need for capital expenditure on updated production equipment and machinery may restrict the amounts and timings of outgoings in other areas, potentially across *all* budgets.

If relevant to you, carry out any amendments to your budget forecast after calculating precisely what these knock-on effects might be in financial terms upon your types, amounts and timings of revenue and expenditure, as appropriate. It may be necessary to liaise further with fellow budget holders and your immediate colleagues within the department or section before doing this. Resubmit your revised forecast to the budget officer, chief accountant or whomever in plenty of time, so that the master budget can be compiled – and individual budgets then set – at the earliest opportunity.

Study the minutes of the meeting as and when they are subsequently produced and circulated – reading them both as a matter of courtesy *and* as a checklist of what has and is expected to happen.

These should detail in particular where and when the committee meeting was held, who chaired and participated in it, the main proposals and points of any discussions, the decisions made, actions to be taken and the date, time and place of the next meeting, if appropriate. Finally, review your performance before, during and after the meeting. The action checklist reproduced as Figure 4.5 will help you to do this.

It is advisable to review your performance before, during and after a budget committee meeting so that you learn from your mistakes, and can make improvements next time around. Answering the following questions should point you in the right direction.

	Yes	No		Yes	No
Did you find out as much as possible about the committee meeting before attending it?	☐	☐	Did your facial expressions match what you were saying?	☐	☐
Did you think carefully about the other participants?	☐	☐	Did you maintain regular eye contact with everyone?	☐	☐
Were the topics for discussion studied in some detail?	☐	☐	Was your body language appropriate too?	☐	☐
Did you consider fully what you had to do at the meeting?	☐	☐	Were your handouts a success?	☐	☐
Was a speech or presentation prepared conscientiously?	☐	☐	Did you use a flipchart effectively?	☐	☐
Was it rehearsed thoroughly?	☐	☐	Was the overhead projector handled well?	☐	☐
Did you contemplate contents, style, equipment and length at rehearsals?	☐	☐	Did you listen carefully to what other participants said?	☐	☐
Was everyone around you aware of the meeting?	☐	☐	Did you make notes, when relevant?	☐	☐
Did you arrive on time?	☐	☐	Were questions asked only as and when appropriate?	☐	☐
Was your appearance suitable for the meeting?	☐	☐	Did you consequently amend your budget forecast in the light of information gained at the meeting?	☐	☐
Did you feel comfortable?	☐	☐	Did you liaise further with colleagues, if necessary?	☐	☐
Were you heard clearly and fully?	☐	☐	Was the adjusted forecast resubmitted as promptly as possible?	☐	☐
Did you make yourself understood?	☐	☐	Were the minutes of the meeting read fully?	☐	☐

Figure 4.5   Attending a budget committee meeting: an action checklist

Developing the master budget

In many (if not most) businesses, the master budget will be drawn up after the budget forecasts have been submitted and discussed, but before individual budgets are finalised. Inevitably, there will be some further discussions with certain budget holders around this time, to ensure that all budgets complement and co-ordinate with each other.

It is helpful to know something about the component parts of a master budget, since these may have a significant impact on the particular budget you are expected to work within and towards. The three key components are:

- the budgeted profit and loss account
- the cash budget
- the budgeted balance sheet.

The budgeted profit and loss account

The master budget could be described as being the last stage of the financial planning function *and* the first stage of the control function. In essence, it is the acid test of the overall viability of the individual budget forecasts – do they combine to create an acceptable profit, cashflow and balance of assets and liabilities at the end of the period? Budget committees in some firms will start the process of compiling a master budget by pulling together all the separate budget forecasts into a profit budget – essentially to see whether or not the firm will make an acceptable profit, if everything unfolds as predicted by the various departmental and sectional budget holders.

A profit budget is simply a document which outlines the estimated sales, direct costs, indirect costs and profits or losses of a business over a specified period of time. Typically, it will cover the forthcoming calendar or accounting year, and will be sub-divided by months. An example of a basic, profit budget form is reproduced as Figure 4.6. Note that this particular example only spans a six-month period whereas 12 months would be the norm.

Looking closely at this profit budget form – which is much the same as any other, ignoring cosmetic differences – 'Sales' will be switched over from the sales budget, with anticipated monthly invoiced sales being noted in the budget boxes across the page. 'Less: Direct costs' consists of two lines here – 'Cost of materials' and 'Wages'. The 'Cost of materials' which makes up each month's invoiced sales includes raw materials, component parts and (in some businesses) packaging and delivery charges too. Details are taken from the purchases and production budget forecasts. The 'Wages' of all the staff associated with buying, making or providing goods will then be noted from the production or personnel budget, depending on where the firm details this.

Deducting 'Direct costs' from 'Sales' leaves 'Gross profit', which will duly be filled out across the page. 'Gross profit margin' – highlighting the relationship between sales and profits – can then be deduced by dividing gross profit by sales and multiplying by 100. The resulting figure shows whether or not the business is buying and selling in an efficient and profitable manner. Most trades and industries have an average gross profit margin against which the firm can compare its performance, and decide if changes need to be made; to prices, cost levels, and the like.

Next, the 'Overheads' are listed – those indirect costs incurred in administering and running the business, regardless of the number of goods produced or services provided. Sub-categories here will differ from one company to another, with some listing by function, department or section (administration, finance, personnel and so on) and others by item (salaries, rent, rates, water and so forth), as illustrated. The choice depends largely upon the preferences of the particular firm. The estimated, annual cost of each individual entry – be it by function or item – is totted up with details being transferred from the various budgets, and placed in the 'Totals' column.

Taking the 'Salaries' total for the period, this is then divided by 12 (or by however many sub-sections exist) with the resultant, matching figures being put in the monthly budget boxes. The same is then done with rent, rates, water and so forth. *When* the various items are to be paid is irrelevant in a profit budget as this document is concerned wholly with identifying whether or not the business is trading profitably. (An assessment of when expenditure is paid out, income is received, the relationship between them and its consequences is made later on, when the cash budget is compiled.) Totalling each monthly column should produce 12 identical 'Total overheads' boxes.

Subtracting the monthly 'Total overheads' from the 'Gross profit' figures leaves the all-important 'Trading profit', which indicates if the business is truly profitable or not. The 'Less depreciation' line shown needs to be completed if any major capital assets are owned, which depreciate in value each year. The simplest way of deducing an annual figure for depreciation is to take the cost of each asset and divide it by the number of years it is expected to last. Adding up the respective annual depreciation figures for all assets and dividing by 12 enables this line to be filled in.

PROFIT BUDGET	Month:			Month:			Month:		
	Est.	Act.	Var.	Est.	Act.	Var.	Est.	Act.	Var.
Sales (A)									
Less: Direct costs									
Cost of materials									
Wages									
Gross profit (B)									
Gross profit margin (B ÷ A x 100%)									
Overheads:									
Salaries									
Rent, rates, water									
Insurance									
Repairs, renewals									
Heat, light, power									
Postage									
Printing, stationery									
Transport									
Telephone									
Professional fees									
Interest charges									
Other									
Total overheads (C)									
Trading profit (B–C)									
Less depreciation									
Net profit before tax									

Figure 4.6   Profit budget form: a basic example

Month:			Month:			Month:			Month:		
Est.	Act.	Var.	Est.	Act.	Var.	Est.	Act.	Var.	Est.	Act.	Var.

Deducting depreciation from trading profit gives the 'Net profit before tax'. The figures across the form are then added together to complete the 'Totals' column on the right, with the exception of the 'Gross profit margin' line which is totalled and divided by 12 to give the average, annual figure. (Further examples of a profit budget and the consequent profit and loss account which derives from it are included in Case study 4.2 on page 103–5.)

From the facts and figures set out within the profit budget, it is relatively easy to compose the budgeted profit and loss account, which is the first of the three main documents of the master budget. To define it, this is a financial statement which specifies the anticipated sales, total costs and profits or losses of a business over a particular period of time, normally one year. Figure 4.7 is an example of a budgeted profit and loss account (Figure 1.7 gave an example earlier).

'Sales' are placed at the top of the statement, with the total figure being taken from the sales and profit budgets. 'Cost of sales' – a sum equal to the cost of materials noted in the profit budget – is then deducted. It is shown in this statement as 'Opening stock' plus 'Purchases' minus 'Closing stock' with the various figures being switched across from the production, purchases and profit budgets compiled previously. 'Sales' less 'Cost of sales' leaves the 'Gross profit', or 'Gross loss' in extreme and unusual circumstances.

Expected 'Overheads' are listed next, sometimes by function, department or section (administration, personnel and the like) or by item (salaries, rent and so on), as illustrated in Figure 4.7. Evidently, data is accumulated from all budgets, including the profit budget. The precise sub-headings used depends on the individual company's preferences – as a rough and ready rule, small firms tend to list items whereas larger ones group by function, or whatever. The ability to monitor the items regularly and accurately is of prime significance here.

Some businesses will list the numerous overheads in a standardised order – often the same sequence that exists in the profit budget – whilst others will do it according to the amounts of money spent on them, with the one incurring the greatest expenditure at the top and the remainder going downwards from there. The difference is largely a cosmetic one. Subtracting the 'Total' overheads from the 'Gross profit' provides a 'Net profit' (or perhaps 'Net loss') figure. This should match the one in the profit budget.

	£	£
Sales		733,000
Opening stock	82,000	
Purchases	406,000	
Closing stock	68,000	
Cost of sales		420,000
Gross profit		**313,000**
Overheads:		
Salaries	106,000	
Rent, rates, water	38,000	
Repairs, renewals	14,000	
Professional fees	6,500	
Interest charges	2,800	
Depreciation	2,700	
Heat, light, power	2,700	
Transport	2,600	
Printing, stationery	1,900	
Postage	1,800	
Insurance	1,700	
Telephone	1,400	
Total		**182,100**
Net profit		**130,900**

Figure 4.7   Budgeted profit and loss account

The cash budget

The cash budget – or cashflow forecast to use another, equally popular name – shows
how cash will flow into and out of a firm over a given period of time, usually one year.
Many, larger businesses do not compile a cash budget – or at least do not formalise it as
part of the overall, master budget – often because of the broad and diverse nature of
their operations and the consequent complexities of doing so. For smaller firms, it is

essential (and in theory, equally so for all concerns) as it is necessary to know that they are not only operating profitably, but also that there are always sufficient cash reserves available to keep trading.

As a common example of what happens to a small business, it will sell its products and services in sufficient quantities but has to wait several months to receive payments. Meanwhile, direct and indirect costs continue to have to be paid. Eventually – with expenditure continually preceding revenue – the cash is used up, and the business is forced to stop trading. An example of a straightforward cash budget form is shown as Figure 4.8 (pages 100–1). It covers six months, although a 12-month budget is more usual.

Referring to this cash budget form – which is broadly similar to most others – it can be seen that 'Receipts' are divided into three categories – 'Cash sales', 'Cash from debtors' (those individuals or organisations which owe the firm money) and 'Capital introduced', which might typically include owners' savings, a bank loan or funds generated by a share issue. All receipts, 'income', 'revenue' or whatever name is used in your company should be put in the appropriate budget boxes according to when they are expected to be received. Each month's budgeted receipts are then added up and the 'Total receipts' line completed.

Then, the 'Payments' are recorded and once more, the sub-headings here will vary from business to business, perhaps being divided up by function, department or section or more likely, by item. The decision depends on the individual firm in question. Data about 'payments to suppliers', 'salaries, wages' and so on will be taken, accumulated and switched across from all of the submitted budget forecasts, with the respective payments, expenditure, outgoings or whatever they are called in your company being placed in the relevant budget boxes depending upon when they are expected to be settled. Each line and monthly column is then added up and the 'Total payments' line and 'Totals' column are filled in.

Subtracting 'Total receipts' from 'Total payments' will leave 'Net cashflow' and hopefully this will be a positive rather than negative figure. As relevant, this will then be added to or deducted from the 'Opening bank balance' to reach the 'Closing bank balance'. This figure then moves forward to become the next month's 'Opening bank balance' and so on, across the page. (Case study 4.2 on pages 103–5 shows the development of a master budget and incorporates another cash budget to be looked at.)

The budgeted balance sheet

The third and final document within a master budget is the budgeted balance sheet. This is a financial statement indicating the firm's assets and liabilities at a given time and showing how its activities have been financed during the preceding period. If completed profit and cash budgets exist, it should be a straightforward task to compose a budgeted balance sheet for the end of the appropriate period. An example of a budgeted balance sheet is shown in Figure 4.9 on page 102 (also Figure 1.8).

Starting at the top of the statement and reading downwards, 'Fixed assets' (or 'Capital assets') are those permanent items of long-term use to a business. These may be divided into three sub-categories – 'tangible' assets like land, buildings, plant, equipment and machinery, 'intangible' assets such as licences, patents and goodwill, plus 'investments' in other companies. Adding together their respective values provides a total figure to be noted.

'Current assets' (or 'Liquid assets') are the ever-changing items which come and go as a business conducts its activities. Typically, these will include stock, work in progress, deposits and pre-payments to other people, cash and debtors; those organisations and individuals who owe money to the firm. 'Current liabilities' are the short-term debts of a business which need to be settled in the next 12 months. These debts might incorporate bank loans and overdrafts, taxes due, deposits and pre-payments by customers and other sums owed to trade and sundry creditors; those organisations and individuals to whom the firm owes money.

Deducting current liabilities from current assets should leave the 'Net current assets' (or 'Working capital') assuming that the concern is trading profitably. If current liabilities exceeded current assets, the resulting deficit would be called the 'Net current liabilities'. Net current assets are added to the fixed assets figure to reach a 'Net assets' figure ('Net worth' or 'Total capital employed'). Had net current liabilities been recorded and exceeded the total value of fixed assets, then a 'Net liabilities' figure would be noted instead.

CASH BUDGET	Month:			Month:			Month:		
Receipts:	Est.	Act.	Var.	Est.	Act.	Var.	Est.	Act.	Var.
Cash sales									
Cash from debtors									
Capital introduced									
Total receipts (A)									
Payments:									
Payments to suppliers									
Salaries, wages									
Rent, rates, water									
Insurance									
Repairs, renewals									
Heat, light, power									
Postage									
Printing, stationery									
Transport									
Telephone									
Professional fees									
Capital payments									
Interest charges									
Other									
VAT payable									
Total payments (B)									
Net cashflow (A–B)									
Opening bank balance									
Closing bank balance									

Figure 4.8   Cash budget form: a straightforward example

Month:			Month:			Month:			Month:		
Est.	Act.	Var.	Est.	Act.	Var.	Est.	Act.	Var.	Est.	Act.	Var.

Fixed assets:	
Leasehold premises	75,000
Equipment, machinery	52,000
Vehicles	17,000
Licences	15,000
	159,000
Current assets:	
Stock, work in progress	30,000
Deposits, pre-payments	10,000
Cash	4,000
Debtors	4,000
	48,000
Current liabilities:	
Taxation	13,000
Trade creditors	12,000
Sundry creditors	9,000
	34,000
Net current assets	14,000
Net assets	173,000
Represented by:	
Share capital	70,000
Profit and loss account	103,000
	173,000

Figure 4.9   Budgeted balance sheet

Below or alongside these various figures – depending on whether a 'vertical' or 'horizontal' format has been chosen for the statement – will be a 'Financed by' (or 'Represented by') section. This states how the trading activities for that period have been funded. Normally, finance will have come from owners' capital, long-term loans and profits generated by those activities (and recorded in the profit budget and profit and loss account). The total figure should be the same as the 'net assets' – hence, the 'balance' in the name 'balance sheet'. (See the worked-through example shown as Case study 4.2 for another budgeted balance sheet.)

CASE STUDY 4.2	**Developing a master budget**

Following the budget committee meeting at which all of the budget forecasts were presented, discussed and agreed, it was the responsibility of Cathy, co-owner of Newbabes Limited, to take away the documents and accumulated notes and prepare a master budget from them. To begin with, she wanted to be sure that the business was profitable if revenues and expenditure were as planned, so she sketched out a rough and ready profit budget, followed by a profit and loss account. Her original notes looked like this:

	October	*November*	*December*	*January*
Sales revenues	130,000	132,000	132,000	128,000
Less materials	38,500	39,000	39,000	37,500
Less wages	42,000	42,000	42,000	42,000
Gross profit	49,500	51,000	51,000	48,500
Less Marketing	5,000	5,000	5,000	5,000
Administration	2,500	2,500	2,500	2,500
Distribution	4,500	4,500	4,500	4,500
Finance	2,000	2,000	2,000	2,000
Personnel	21,000	21,000	21,000	21,000
Depreciation	1,000	1,000	1,000	1,000
Total	36,000	36,000	36,000	36,000
Net profit	13,500	15,000	15,000	12,500
Sales				1,587,000
Opening stock	160,000			
Direct costs	963,000			
Closing stock	190,000			
Cost of sales				933,000
Gross profit				654,000
Overheads:				
Personnel	252,000			
Marketing	60,000			
Distribution	54,000			
Administration	30,000			
Finance	24,000			
Depreciation	12,000			
Total				432,000
Net profit				222,000

▶

From these, Cathy could see that profits were acceptable for the year. They were up on the previous period by some 8 per cent – well ahead of the inflation rate which she had aimed to match or slightly better. However, Cathy was also concerned about the firm's cash position during the year, wanting to make sure that it remained in (substantial) credit throughout this time. Also, she wished to check on their projected assets and liabilities at the close of the period. Hence, she referred again to the budgets given to her in order to produce the following (draft) cash budget and budgeted balance sheet:

	April	May	June	July
Sales income	146,000	140,000	140,000	142,000
Other income	—	—	—	—
Total income	146,000	140,000	140,000	142,000
Production	76,900	89,300	89,500	89,900
Marketing	4,000	8,000	4,000	8,000
Administration	2,400	2,400	2,700	2,700
Distribution	4,300	4,700	4,500	4,900
Finance	1,800	1,800	2,000	2,200
Personnel	22,000	22,000	23,000	22,000
Capital	22,000	—	8,000	2,200
Total outgoings	133,400	128,200	133,700	131,900
Net cashflow	+12,600	+11,800	+6,300	+10,100
Opening balance	12,000	24,600	36,400	42,700
Closing balance	24,600	36,400	42,700	52,800

Fixed assets:	
Freehold property	82,000
Equipment, machinery	110,000
Vehicles	11,000
	203,000
Current assets:	
Stock, work in progress	197,000
Cash	17,000
Debtors	137,000
	351,000
Current liabilities:	
Taxation	42,000
Trade creditors	67,000
Sundry creditors	69,000
	178,000
Net current assets	173,000
Net assets	376,000
Financed by:	
Owners' funds	154,000
Profits	222,000
	376,000

Evidently, the overall master budget looked very favourable in the circumstances, with acceptable profits being generated, a positive cashflow at all times and substantial assets at the year-end – thus enabling 'Newbabes' to proceed with its plans to diversify into new products and markets. Having made a couple of adjustments to her own capital expenditure budget so that cash resources remained high enough throughout, the various forecasts given to Cathy were approved as budgets.

SUMMARY

1 A budget committee plays a central role in the budgetary process;

(a) Typically, it will comprise representatives of executive management and the accounting function as well as senior budget holders.

(b) Its activities include setting the budget period and sub-periods, revenue and expenditure categories and sub-categories, general guidelines and budget assumptions, studying budget forecasts at meetings, creating a master budget and supervising developments thereafter.

2 Most budget holders will be expected to present their budget forecasts to a committee meeting.

(a) Before the meeting, it is sensible to discover as much as possible about it, the other participants and topics for discussion and to prepare and rehearse a speech thoroughly, if relevant.

(b) During the meeting, budget holders should concentrate on making an effective speech, using equipment properly and being a good participant. The meeting is a team effort, not a divisive free-for-all.

(c) Afterwards, it is wise to deal promptly with any activities that need to be done, such as amending the budget forecast, reading the minutes and reviewing the meeting.

3 A master budget will be developed after the budget forecasts have been submitted. It comprises:

(a) A budgeted profit and loss account specifying the anticipated sales, total costs and profits or losses of a business over a particular period of time.

(b) A cash budget which shows how cash is expected to flow into and out of a concern over a specific period.

(c) A budgeted balance sheet indicating the firm's assets and liabilities at a given moment and showing how its activities over the preceding period were financed.

To adhere to the budget – or at least to highlight that it is not possible – you need to establish monitoring procedures which are easy to administer, regular and completed at the lowest level.

CHAPTER FIVE

How to keep track of budgets

- ■ Establishing monitoring procedures
- ■ Studying revenues
- ■ Checking expenditure
- ■ Summary

Having had your sales, production, capital expenditure or departmental budget approved as it stands or amended in accordance with the overall master budget, you should now be in a position to move on and actually monitor it on a weekly, monthly or quarterly basis, as appropriate. To do this effectively, you need to establish suitable monitoring procedures and ensure that you and/or (perhaps more likely) your team know how to study revenues and check expenditure as and when necessary so that you are able to fill in the budget form properly at the set intervals.

Establishing monitoring procedures

In theory, once a budget has been finalised, its revenues *must* be achieved and expenditure *must not* be exceeded. Of course, this is rarely a wholly realistic goal as internal and external circumstances can and do change and will have some impact on your budget, for better or worse. In practice therefore, budgets are (or certainly should be) subject to constant review and may be adjusted at a subsequent, budget committee meeting. Nonetheless, this official goal is still something to be worked towards – otherwise there is little point in setting a budget in the first place.

To help adhere to the budget – or at least to highlight that it is not possible – you need to establish monitoring procedures which are:

- easy to administer

- regular

- completed at the lowest level.

Easy to administer

It is essential that revenues, expenditure and the consequent profits and cashflow can be monitored easily and swiftly rather than being a difficult and time-consuming process. Hence, the data needed to monitor finances – taken from sales invoices, receipts, books, ledgers and the like – must be available under the same category and sub-category headings as those used in your budget form, such as 'postage' and 'stationery', for example. Hopefully, it will not take the too detailed 'elastic bands' and 'paper clips' approach, as excessive information can be unnecessary and wasteful. More time and money would be spent on collecting and perusing the details than might be saved by the elimination of identified problems.

Just as important, data has to be readily accessible *and* available whenever it is required. In some instances, it may need to be taken at source, direct from sales invoices, receipts and so forth – perhaps when cashflow is poor and is being watched closely each week, or even daily. On other occasions, it will be noted from company records, books, ledgers and so on. It is imperative that these records are compiled as fast, as accurately and as clearly as is necessary for budgetary purposes. Evidently, the details must be there, full and complete, when the next budget column is being filled out.

Regular

Assuming that the data concerning revenues and expenditure are available when they are wanted, then the question of how often it should be checked (and the budget monitored) has to be addressed – with the answer being determined by the nature of your particular business circumstances. Once a month is fairly commonplace, although you must be flexible enough to shorten or lengthen these times if your individual situation changes substantially.

Completed at the lowest level

The efficient monitoring of a budget usually involves control beginning at the lowest possible level of the business organisation – that is, where the revenue was received or the expenditure incurred. As examples, sales representatives who make cash sales on their journeys and office juniors who take petty cash to buy stationery must be instructed (and reminded regularly if necessary) to record and/or pass on these financial facts (and supporting documentation) as appropriate, feeding them into the company's record system in the required manner. Each member of the team within a particular section or department must be aware of their responsibilities in this area.

Effective monitoring tends to follow the 'management by exception' approach, whereby the budget holder has full knowledge of his or her individual budget as set by the budget committee (and perhaps partial or even complete understanding of others and the master budget, depending on company circumstances). However, day-to-day, week-by-week revenues and expenditure received, incurred and recorded by sales representatives, office juniors and other employees will not be drawn to his or her attention, unless they differ significantly from expectations.

> The efficient monitoring of a budget usually involves control beginning at the lowest possible level of the business organisation – that is, where the revenue was received or the expenditure incurred.

Thus, that sales representative may make a point of notifying the departmental manager that a major sales order has been cancelled, whereas having had one or two items dropped from it would not be commented on.

In this way, your time will be kept free for you to concentrate on other, more important budget (and non-budget) activities, rather than being tied up with relatively trivial matters which often do little more than confirm that the budget is progressing as anticipated (or as near to it as makes no difference). Of course, the point at which differences – or 'variances' – are considered to be 'significant' and worthy of being referred up to you will vary from one business to another. A variation of (plus or minus) 10 per cent in amounts (and indeed timings) is often the decisive point in most firms. Clearly, everyone has to know what is termed 'significant', if this approach is to work properly.

You too will probably be expected to adopt the same, 'management by exception' approach to your involvement in the monitoring of your budget. Typically, you will study revenue and check expenditure figures at source or from company records on a monthly basis or whenever, consequently filling in the 'actual' column of your budget form, comparing them to the 'estimated' figures and then filling out the 'variance' column as appropriate. Minor and reversible variances should be handled by you, whilst major and potentially damaging ones must be brought to the attention of the budget committee or budget officer, as relevant.

Examples of the reports used to do this are shown as Figures 5.1 and 5.2.

Ultimately, of course, major variances which cannot be dealt with by you or the budget committee working together in unison will have to be accepted – for example, the market is diminishing, and customers' businesses are closing down *and* far more rapidly than was ever expected. It is in irreversible decline. Thus, the sales, related budgets and the master budget will have to be revised – and *fast* as working to an inaccurate budget is pointless, and potentially fatal. In this instance, production schedules would be maintained and capital items purchased perhaps, without the necessary revenues coming in to justify them.

Studying revenues

To monitor the budget effectively, each revenue line and column (and then, every line and column of expenditure) needs to be looked at regularly with details being noted at source, transferred to company books and records and referred to thereafter before being switched over to the budget form in due course.

If appropriate in your situation, you and your team should study revenues with regard to:

- types
- amounts
- timings.

Types

Evidently, the revenues that will (hopefully) be coming in will vary according to the budget you are managing – although income from the sale of goods and/or services is most likely. Whether these have been divided up by product group, sales representatives' territories or marketplace, you need to monitor them in the same ways that they are listed on the form. Data has to be filed punctually and accurately, with invoices, sales receipts, remittance advices, records of takings and the like all being grouped in the agreed manner and transferred to books and ledgers with apropriate keys being placed alongside of entries for easy identification – 'WAY 1' for 'Wayfarer One', 'AD' for 'Administration Department', 'NE' for 'North East', or whatever.

Other types of revenue may be applicable as well, depending on your circumstances – capital might be raised by a share issue (with some or all of the proceeds perhaps being allocated across several departments and budgets) or the sale of outdated or unwanted assets such as buildings, plant, equipment and machinery. Again, details need to be noted promptly and fully with documents being categorised within the established sub-headings and records kept with identifying marks for quick and easy reference, whenever necessary.

Amounts

Day-to-day, week-by-week or month after month – depending on your individual situation – the respective amounts of revenue must be noted from direct or secondary sources with data being placed in the appropriate lines and columns, in turn. Consequently, the 'variance' boxes must be completed too, thus highlighting the differences between budgeted and actual revenues. Relatively insignificant variances – such as those of less than 10 per cent – may be allowed to go unchecked or commented upon if they are one-offs which are easily understood, are not likely to have any (long-term) impact or can be resolved by the budget holder and/or his or her team.

VARIATION REPORT:		Period:			Year to date:			Reason(s) for variance(s)
Revenues:		*Est.*	*Act.*	*Var.*	*Est.*	*Act.*	*Var.*	
Product	Volume							
	Price							
	Value							
Product	Volume							
	Price							
	Value							
Product	Volume							
	Price							
	Value							
Product	Volume							
	Price							
	Value							
Product	Volume							
	Price							
	Value							
Product	Volume							
	Price							
	Value							
Other	Volume							
	Price							
	Value							
Other	Volume							
	Price							
	Value							
Department:					Name:			
Date:					Signature:			

Figure 5.1   Variation report: revenue variances

VARIATION REPORT:		Period:			Year to date:			Reason(s) for variance(s)
Expenditure:		Est.	Act.	Var.	Est.	Act.	Var.	
Start-up	Volume							
	Price							
	Value							
Start-up	Volume							
	Price							
	Value							
Direct	Volume							
	Price							
	Value							
Direct	Volume							
	Price							
	Value							
Indirect	Volume							
	Price							
	Value							
Indirect	Volume							
	Price							
	Value							
Capital	Volume							
	Price							
	Value							
Capital	Volume							
	Price							
	Value							
Department:					Name:			
Date:					Signature:			

Figure 5.2   Variation report: expenditure variances

Timings

Often, budget holders concentrate almost exclusively on the amounts of revenues an-ticipated and received with substantial variances being attributed to a cancelled order, the closure of a major customer's firm, and the like. However, the timings of the receipt of revenues can be a major factor and the cause of some variances – quite simply, payments to your concern are made much later (or occasionally much earlier) than expected. Overall, sales and profit levels may remain in line with budget expectations but cashflow is different, sometimes quite noticeably, and most likely for the worse. It is important to be able to distinguish between variances which are caused by differing amounts *and* by timings. Figure 5.3 is an action checklist for studying revenues. Case study 5.1 examines revenue variances.

When studying revenues, it can be helpful to have a checklist of points that you can tick off as and when they have been considered:

	Yes	No		Yes	No
Have you checked the sales per product group?	☐	☐	Have you perused the sales per marketplace?	☐	☐
Their amounts?	☐	☐	Their amounts too?	☐	☐
Their timings?	☐	☐	Timings as well?	☐	☐
By referring to direct sources?	☐	☐	With data obtained from direct sources?	☐	☐
By looking at secondary sources?	☐	☐	Also from secondary ones?	☐	☐
Have you studied the sales per sales representative's territory?	☐	☐	Have you assessed the other types of revenue?	☐	☐
The amounts?	☐	☐	The amounts involved?	☐	☐
The timings?	☐	☐	The timings?	☐	☐
With details being taken from direct sources?	☐	☐	Using direct sources?	☐	☐
From secondary ones?	☐	☐	Drawing on secondary sources?	☐	☐

Figure 5.3   Studying revenues: an action checklist

CASE STUDY 5.1 **Recognising revenue variances**

Mary's role within the Newbabes organisation was a key one as she was responsible for maintaining sales revenues and making sure that they were as expected, as well as recognising major variances, rectifying them whenever and as soon as possible and alerting her colleagues to difficulties as and when appropriate. Her two assistants – Malcolm and Helen – were instructed to record and file all incoming orders according to type (multiple, northern independent and so forth) on a 'same day' basis. They also had to liaise closely with Cathy's financial assistant – Rebecca – who noted incoming payments, so that revenue timings were recorded accurately. Any 'significant' problems – defined as a reduced order from a multiple or *any* cancelled order – had to be referred to Mary straightaway. Otherwise, she received data at the end of each month.

The first three months of the 1998–9 trading year went smoothly and according to plan. Mary was given and then sorted revenue details into eight categories – one for each of the four multiples, with the remaining ones covering the independents in the north, east, south and west. She felt that these particular categories allowed greater analysis and identification of problems in advance to take place than the old 12 regional divisions did – and she was subsequently proved correct. Mary noted the amounts in the 'estimated' columns, putting variances (such as they were) in the adjacent columns, as appropriate. The timing of payments was as predicted. All was well.

Then, a potentially serious problem started to develop – and only Mary's well-structured budget format and attention to detail enabled her to spot it at an early stage. Overall, the amounts of revenue being received increased – mainly due to larger orders being placed and paid for promptly by one of the multiples. Simultaneously, the timings of payments from various independents in the north and east began to slow. These were not drawn swiftly to Mary's attention as the increase was viewed as beneficial by the two assistants and the delays seen as being relatively unimportant, given their individual nature. Also, the combined effect of some payments being late and others being larger than expected and paid quickly was to create the impression that all was proceeding to plan. Basically, they cancelled each other out!

Fortunately, Mary spotted the variances. Dividing revenues into those eight categories allowed her to see that the increased sales were coming from just one multiple and that there were payment delays within the northern and eastern independent categories. She was not unduly concerned about the multiple's additional purchases – they were not large enough to put undue pressure on production and she was aware from talks with the buyer that subsequent orders would be correspondingly lower anyway. Also, a rise in stock levels built into the production budget was designed to absorb highs such as this, and lows too.

However, the late payments from some independents were of greater concern – although these were disguised at present by the multiple's activities, they would become very apparent and cause significant cashflow problems later on, once that multiple's purchasing patterns had levelled off as they were due to do. Given the way in which figures were accumulated by category and daily, Mary was able to monitor the situation individually, day to day. Discussions with Cathy followed by several phone calls to the independents concerned did improve the situation, bringing it back in line with expectations.

Checking expenditure

Equally important when monitoring a budget – if not more so in many instances – is the need to check expenditure regularly, on a line-by-line, column-to-column basis.

As with revenues, it is sensible to approach this on-going task by viewing it in three ways:

- types
- amounts
- timings.

Types

The expenditure that you incur during the period will depend on your specific budget – whether production, capital expenditure or a departmental one such as for finance or administration. Similarly, the ways in which they are sub-categorised will vary too, probably according to the tradition and preferences of the business organisation you are working for – 'start-up', 'direct', 'indirect' and 'capital expenditure' are relatively commonplace groupings (albeit under slightly different names in some cases) although a lengthier list of items of expenditure may be preferred, perhaps in your firm.

Whatever the situation, details must be accumulated carefully with employees filling in time sheets, stock issue and transfer notes, vehicle journey records, petty cash vouchers, advances on expenses forms and similar documentation promptly and collecting invoices, receipts and so on, as instructed. Key data then needs to be transferred properly to job cost sheets, manufacturing reports, weekly records of cash payments, cheques issued and bank transactions, all under the agreed headings and as and when required. Relevant keys – 'SU' for start-up, 'PR' for printing and so forth – may be incorporated within these books too.

Amounts

Each and every day, week or month as relevant, the various amounts of expenditure have to be lifted from direct sources such as invoices and receipts and/or secondary sources like the weekly record of bank transactions with the accumulated and totalled data being noted in the lines and columns, as appropriate. Then, actual amounts can be deducted from estimated sums with any positive or negative variances being recorded in the relevant 'variance' boxes. As with revenue variances, those which are considered to be insignificant by the firm will not need to be reported upwards if they are unlikely to be repeated, have a knock-on effect or can be remedied swiftly by the budget holder and the team.

Timings

It is essential that not only the amounts but also the timings of expenditure are studied too, and any variances noted and consequently dealt with, as appropriate. As with the receipt of revenues, the early or late payment of expenditure can have a major impact on variances. By and large, profit levels will remain the same whether an item is purchased two months earlier or later than planned (assuming it remains within the set budget period) but cashflow will be affected, often dramatically. Figure 5.4 is an action checklist for checking expenditure. Case study 5.2 illustrates how to recognise expenditure variances.

When checking expenditure, you may find it helps to refer to a list of points that can be marked off once they have been looked at carefully:

	Yes	No		Yes	No
Have you checked start-up expenditure?	☐	☐	Heat, light, power?	☐	☐
			Insurance?	☐	☐
Drawings?	☐	☐	Repairs, maintenance?	☐	☐
Specifications?	☐	☐			
			Postage?	☐	☐
Production line?	☐	☐	Printing?	☐	☐
Rewriting literature?	☐	☐			
			Stationery?	☐	☐
Reprinting literature?	☐	☐	Advertising, promotion?	☐	☐
Other?	☐	☐			
			Telephone?	☐	☐
Have you considered direct expenditure?	☐	☐	Transport?	☐	☐
Raw materials?	☐	☐	Professional fees?	☐	☐
Component parts?	☐	☐	Finance charges?	☐	☐
Goods for resale?	☐	☐	Other?	☐	☐
Labour wages?	☐	☐	Have you appraised capital expenditure?	☐	☐
After-sales service?	☐	☐	Land?	☐	☐
Other?	☐	☐	Buildings?	☐	☐
Have you worked through indirect expenditure?	☐	☐	Plant?	☐	☐
Rent?	☐	☐	Equipment?	☐	☐
Rates?	☐	☐	Machinery?	☐	☐
Water?	☐	☐	Vehicles?	☐	☐
			Other?	☐	☐

Figure 5.4   Checking expenditure: an action checklist

CASE STUDY 5.2 **Recognising expenditure variances**

Steve had to monitor production expenditure on a continuing basis to make certain that it was all as anticipated. He was expected to take immediate steps to remedy any variances as they occurred, and before they could cause any damage to his and associated budgets. He had to notify his colleagues of problems which could not be rectified swiftly, or at all. Those employees who worked below him were told to fill in, note and file (copies of) all paperwork as and when generated and to liaise closely with other workers to exchange mutually relevant information. 'Anything out of the ordinary' – to use Steve's words – should be mentioned to him in passing 'however trivial it might seem'. Otherwise, completed books and records should be handed over every month, so the budget could be dealt with fully, and on time.

For nearly six months of the 1998–9 trading period, everything unfolded just as expected. Numerous, trivial differences were brought to Steve's attention which he handled easily – most of these would have irritated many managers, but Steve had a real feel for the nitty-gritty and diverse nature of his budget and recognised the need for attention to detail. At the end of each month, he took the accumulated documentation and transferred it to the 'estimated' and 'variance' boxes within the budget form. All was in order – or so it appeared for some considerable time, until it was almost too late.

The problem arose under the 'materials' heading within the budget which Steve had earlier sub-divided repeatedly into separate lines for each and every raw material and component part with sufficient room for volumes, prices and values to be noted, as appropriate. One of the component parts was a piece of special fabric which enabled babies' bottles to be kept warm longer than when placed in conventional materials – a relatively inexpensive gimmick really, but an integral feature of the changing bag nonetheless. Without it, the product would be incomplete and effectively unsellable. Over the six months, the amounts of material delivered regularly fell short of those ordered, but only by about 5 to 6 per cent each – not enough to be identified straightaway, but sufficient to add up to a noticeable shortfall after a while.

One of Steve's employees had picked up the discrepancy early on and had referred to his counterpart in distribution who had said that stocks were 'ample at present'. Subsequently, he thought no more about it when these discrepancies occurred again. Thus, it was left to Steve to spot the accumulated (and by now substantial) variance at a later stage which he was only able to do because of the way in which he had broken down his budget and monitored it so conscientiously, month in and month out. The shortfall – which would have reduced production to a standstill within weeks – could then be rectified by placing a substantial order immediately, and sending those careless employees to collect it!

SUMMARY

1 To monitor a budget effectively, suitable monitoring procedures must be established and everyone needs to know how revenues and expenditure are studied and checked so that the budget form can be completed properly.

2 Monitoring procedures should be:

- easy to administer
- regular
- completed at the lowest level

3 Each revenue line and column must be filled in at set intervals with data being taken at source or from other company records. Revenues should be considered with regard to:

- types
- amounts
- timings

4 Every expenditure line and column has to be filled out regularly with figures being transferred from appropriate company documents and records. Expenditure should be evaluated in terms of:

- types
- amounts
- timings

When working within and towards a budget,
accept that – however careful and thorough the planning
stage may have been – your budget is still based on 'ifs,
buts and maybes'.

CHAPTER SIX

How to adhere to budgets

- Identifying significant variances

- Achieving revenues

- Controlling expenditure

- Making changes

- Summary

Given the differing amounts and timings of revenues and expenditure – either before or whenever you fill in the appropriate 'estimated', 'actual' and 'variance' columns – you have to know what to do to ensure that you can maintain your budget, as planned. You need to be able to identify significant variances and recognise how to deal with them so that revenues are consequently achieved and expenditure controlled in line with expectations. Alternatively, problems will need to be referred upwards and changes made to this, other budgets and the master budget.

Identifying significant variances

When working within and towards a budget, it is essential to accept the fact that however careful and thorough the planning stage may have been, your budget is still based to some extent on 'ifs, buts and maybes'. There is always an element of subjectivity and guesswork involved. Similarly, internal and external circumstances do change unexpectedly and have a positive or (more often) negative impact. Thus, the budget can rarely be wholly accurate, if at all. Significant variances – generally defined as being 10 per cent above or below expectations – should not necessarily be seen as a failure.

To begin with, it is important that you actually spot variances, categorise them and then try to calculate their causes in your particular circumstances – later on you can set about assessing their likely, knock-on effects on your and other budgets and how to remedy them.

Most variances can be categorised in the following ways, with the final, somewhat unusual, category requiring as much attention as the rest:

- revenue–price variance
- revenue–volume variance
- revenue–timing variance
- expenditure–price variance
- expenditure–volume variance
- expenditure–timing variance
- no significant variances.

Revenue–price variance

Clearly, any noticeable variances in revenue received is of primary concern – not only to the immediate budget holder but to the entire company as most budgetary systems are revenue-initiated and -driven. Sales revenue – the main or, in many cases, exclusive source of funds for firms – may go down or up because of price cuts or rises. Typically, prices may have had to be reduced more than expected to help a product become established in an overseas market. Other revenue – from a share issue, perhaps – may be lower or higher than anticipated. Possibly, the planned share issue price was increased as the company's reputation improved in the run up to the issue.

Revenue–volume variance

This is probably the most common variance of all, especially for sales revenue where the number of units sold or services provided are fewer (or occasionally more) than expected. For example, a leading customer's business may have been forced to close, with little or no warning provided. Alternatively, several new customers could have started trading with your firm. Other revenue – such as that from the sale of unwanted capital items – might have fluctuated in terms of volume too. Some items of equipment might not have attracted the interest that was predicted. Conversely, a larger piece of land might have been sold off.

Revenue–timing variance

Often overlooked – particularly at sectional or departmental budget level where the importance of a positive cashflow is not always so apparent – is the question of the timing of the revenue obtained. In some instances, it may be received earlier – perhaps more customers than expected take advantage of a new, prompt-payment discount structure, or a share issue is brought forward to coincide with unexpected, favourable publicity. On other occasions, it will be obtained later – generally deteriorating economic conditions persuading customers to hold on to their money for much longer, as a typical example.

Expenditure–price variance

For the majority of budget holders, significant variances in expenditure will be of equal if not greater concern than those relating to revenues. After all, most budgets within a company are mainly or exclusively expenditure-based. The price of items or services bought under the headings of start-up, direct, indirect and/or capital expenditure (or whatever) may simply be higher or (less likely) lower than indicated in the budget – those raw materials and component

> Often overlooked – particularly at sectional or departmental budget level where the importance of a positive cashflow is not always so apparent – is the question of the timing of the revenue obtained.

parts imported from overseas may go up in price more than anticipated. Possibly the cost of fuel for heat, light and power might fall unexpectedly because an alternative supplier is found.

Expenditure–volume variance

Often, the prices of goods and services purchased remain much the same as predicted but the quantities used are above or (less frequently) below expected levels – usually this type of variance occurs when a business is being set up, is diversifying into new products and/or markets, and budgets are consequently more subjective than on other occasions. As an example, when starting up a concern, accountants, solicitors, consultants and other professionals may be referred to more than was first planned. Occasionally, quantities used will be less than predicted – for example, labour input into the production of a new line might fall as new technological equipment is mastered and its use maximised.

Expenditure–timing variance

The timing of expenditure is not always considered as fully as it should be at sectional or departmental level, where the overall effect of paying earlier or later than planned is rarely apparent to budget holders there. Expenditure may be paid out sooner than envisaged – perhaps the budget holder stresses the urgent need for updated machinery now in order to maintain productivity. Alternatively, it could be incurred later, perhaps because the budget officer (or whoever) is conscious of the strain that payment will put on cash resources and other budgets' planned expenditure.

No significant variances

Some budgets unfold almost wholly as planned, recording only minor revenue and expenditure variances. It is tempting to assume that the holders of such budgets are extremely skilful, have been fortunate that internal and external circumstances have not conspired against them, and are highly successful. The reality is more likely to be that they have been ultra-cautious, underestimating revenues so that these are always achieved or exceeded slightly whilst overestimating expenditure, with additional purchases being made as necessary near to the end of the period to justify the level of expenditure set, and to ensure it remains at least the same for next year. Figure 6.1 is an action checklist enabling you to assess the reasons for having a budget with no significant variances. Case study 6.1 is a worked-through example of a so-called 'perfect budget'.

It is possible that your budget may unfold exactly as planned, or with only minor, short-term variances of less than 10 per cent. If this happens, you should consider the reasons why. Asking yourself – and then answering – these questions may help you to do this:

■ Are my revenue and/or expenditure figures almost wholly accurate?

■ Are revenue and expenditure prices largely as anticipated?

■ All volumes much as anticipated?

■ All timings virtually the same as estimated?

■ Why is this?

■ Am I especially skilful at budgeting?

■ Was I lucky to a certain degree?

■ Did I consciously underestimate some revenue figures?

■ Did I deliberately overstate some expenditure figures?

■ Why did I do this? To make revenues more achievable? Expenditure easier to control?

■ What are the consequences of these actions for me? To make me look good, perhaps? Impress colleagues?

■ What are the effects of the actions more generally? To mislead colleagues? The budget committee too? To make associated budgets less accurate? Including the all-important master budget?

■ Have I cancelled out the advantages of budgeting? Its role as a plan, an incentive, a control function?

■ Have I increased its disadvantages? Perhaps making the process even slower to be established?

■ What do I need to do to remedy matters?

Figure 6.1   Assessing an accurate budget: an action checklist

---

CASE STUDY 6.1   **The 'perfect budget'**

Of the numerous budgets within Newbabes Limited, only one unfolded almost perfectly, regularly recording variances of less than 10 per cent in terms of volumes, prices and timing – Adam's distribution budget. Whilst his colleagues around him constantly seemed to be tackling (albeit mostly minor) problems in order to remedy variances, he seemed to have to do little more than fill out his budget form every month and note with satisfaction the insignificant variances (if any) that existed there. Eventually, this started to worry him and he decided to take a long, hard look at what was happening.

Initially, he studied closely his expenditure figures – prices, volumes and timings – and saw that they were virtually all as estimated. Adam identified several reasons for this. It was a relatively small and compact budget with a limited number of types of expenditure included within it – and obviously this made it that much easier to predict accurately. His seven years' experience of budgeting in this field had helped him too. He had been lucky as well that volumes, prices and timings had unfolded without a hitch. In retrospect, he had inflated his 'miscellaneous items' volumes somewhat and used this entry for all sorts of minor expenditure which if incorporated elsewhere might have caused some variances to be termed 'significant' on occasions. He decided to keep a closer eye on this in future.

Achieving revenues

Having identified, grouped *and* worked out the causes of variances, you must then move ahead to consider the effects of these variances on this and other budgets, including the master budget.

You should also think about how the variances might be rectified in your particular circumstances. Revenues can be studied in relation to:

- price variances
- volume variances
- timing variances.

Price variances

Revenue–price variance may be sub-divided into four categories for analysis – selling prices of goods and services for sale go up *or* down; prices of other revenue items such as unwanted capital assets are higher *or* lower than anticipated. Obviously, variances in selling prices of products and services for sale tend to be most significant, having both a roll-over effect on the sales budget and knock-on effects on others. Assuming that everything else remains the same – most notably, sales volume, direct and indirect expenditure – then increased selling prices will boost gross profit, net profit and generate more cash. Evidently, the consequences will be reversed if selling prices decrease – so too will profits and immediate cash resources.

An increase in selling prices will generally be regarded as acceptable by most companies if – and it is sometimes a big 'if' – they can be sustained and do not have an adverse effect upon sales volumes. Likewise, a drop in selling prices will be considered to be unacceptable – and the remedies might include raising the prices of goods in other product groups, territories or markets in order to compensate. If this is not possible, attention may be given to nullifying the potential knock-on effects by attempting to improve sales volumes or to reduce direct and perhaps indirect expenditure so that profits and cashflow are maintained.

> Revenue–price variance may be sub-divided into four categories for analysis – selling prices of goods and services for sale go up *or* down; prices of other revenue items such as unwanted capital assets are higher *or* lower than anticipated.

Volume variances

This type of variance can be sub-categorised into four, similar groupings – the number of products and services sold rises *or* falls, the number of other revenue items sold increases *or* decreases. Again, variances in the quantities of goods and services being sold are of greatest significance, given the on-going and knock-on effects of these. If other factors such as selling prices, expenditure prices and volumes stay unchanged then higher sales volumes will normally improve gross profit, net profit in turn and the cash resources available to the company as well. Not surprisingly, if volumes are less, profits will be lower too, and the cashflow situation worsened.

Higher sales volumes will probably be viewed as a positive trend in the majority of companies, assuming that they can cope with the extra demand for goods and services. Reduced volumes are seen as potentially fatal, especially if the downward trend continues for any length of time. Remedies might incorporate the introduction of a discount structure for bulk purchases and an advertising campaign to increase awareness of the product's strengths. If unsuccessful, thought will need to be given to reducing the impact of the variances, possibly by raising selling prices of popular lines, or cutting back on expenditure, thus upholding profits and cash resources.

Timing variances

Revenue–timing variance may be split into two groups – revenues are obtained earlier than estimated and revenues are received later than planned. Essentially, the timing of revenues does not affect the annual profitability of a firm – except indirectly, where, for example, it can be argued that delayed receipts increase the need for overdraft and even loan facilities which incur charges that subsequently reduce net profit. However, it does influence cashflow significantly and therefore, the company's ability to pay its way. All things being equal, earlier receipt of revenues means more cash in the bank, and later receipt means less is available.

Receiving revenues early is usually regarded as a bonus enabling expenditure to be paid on time, whilst later payments are seen as being financially risky, if not potentially fatal, particularly for smaller, cash-conscious firms. There are various ways of trying to speed up payments – more specifically, eliminating delays in the preparation and despatch of invoices, offering appropriate discounts for prompt payments (as long as these do not reduce prompt profits excessively), shortening credit periods allowed and chasing up outstanding debts as vigorously as possible.

With regard to revenue–price, –volume and –timing variances, it is important that you always work through the consequences in relation to your own, individual situation. As an example, increasing the volume of goods and services sold is normally beneficial but is not always. Perhaps the product group that is selling more is a loss leader priced below cost level to entice new customers to buy it. Similarly, greater volumes may put excessive pressure on production facilities which are unable to manufacture goods at the required rate. Also, they can pressurise cash resources as direct costs on raw materials and the like may have to be paid for upfront.

Likewise, it is sensible to take account of the possible effects of any changes you might implement to remedy those variances. For example, introducing early settlement discounts to encourage customers to pay quicker may eliminate timing variances but those taking advantage of such facilities will be paying less, thus increasing price variances and ultimately, reducing profit levels. Cutting credit terms and pursuing debts can alienate and persuade customers to take their business elsewhere – thus affecting price, volume *and* timing variances! An action checklist which may help you to achieve budgeted revenues is shown as Figure 6.2. Case study 6.2 is an example of how to remedy revenue variances.

Identifying significant revenue variances is relatively easy, as long as you study revenue figures conscientiously. Resolving them and achieving revenues is harder, but referring to a checklist of points can at least help you to approach the task thoroughly and in a comprehensive manner:

	Yes	No		Yes	No
Is there a price variance?	☐	☐	To that master budget?	☐	☐
Have you considered its immediate and on-going effects on your budget?	☐	☐	Have you decided how to tackle it?	☐	☐
Other, related budgets?	☐	☐	What will be the knock-on effects of your response?	☐	☐
The master budget?	☐	☐	Do you have a problem with a timing variance?	☐	☐
Do you know how to remedy it?	☐	☐	Do you realise what it is doing to your particular budget?	☐	☐
Have you calculated the consequences of your actions?	☐	☐	To other ones?	☐	☐
Does a volume variance exist?	☐	☐	To the master budget?	☐	☐
Do you recognise what it is doing to your budget, now and in the future?	☐	☐	Have you settled on a course of action to rectify it?	☐	☐
To fellow budgets?	☐	☐	Do you know what the results of this will be?	☐	☐

Figure 6.2 Achieving revenues: an action checklist

CASE STUDY 6.2   **Remedying revenue variances**

Eight months into Newbabes' trading year, Mary's sales budget threatened to go seriously off course – the anticipated lull in sales during months seven and eight (and nine) was some 20 per cent worse than expected. To exacerbate matters, one of the multiples was settling its bills after 90 days, rather than the expected 30. Mary had already raised these issues at a weekly management meeting towards the close of the seventh month and it had been agreed that she would continue to monitor sales closely for the time being with Cathy contacting the multiple for an explanation. By the end of the eighth month – and with the situation much the same – more drastic action was called for.

At the next weekly meeting, Mary raised these problems again, stressing the importance of resolving them promptly by outlining the consequences if they were allowed to continue. With regard to the sales slump, production was currently producing in excess of requirements which was leading to overstocking and in effect, essential cash resources being tied up in slow-moving, dated items. Cashflow was suffering too especially as the costs of (over)-production were being met before (lower) sales income was received – and it was made worse by the delays in payment by that multiple. Even if production levels were adjusted accordingly – as indeed they were beginning to be – it would mean staff being laid off, equipment and machinery being under-used, and so forth. Inevitably, reduced sales eventually mean reduced profits, leaving insufficient funds for capital re-investment, diversification or even continued trade.

A brainstorming session between Mary, Cathy, Steve, Raj and Adam generated numerous ideas for tackling the sales slump, including the introduction of special offers, discounts and so on, to stimulate sales. However, it was felt after lengthy discussions that to introduce these quickly *and* properly would be difficult, might create the impression of desperate measures and, if the firm was encouraged strongly to continue with them by eager multiples, might be a (financial) burden in the future. Perhaps surprisingly, Cathy and Steve – who had seen all this many times before – decided that they should simply 'hold tight', reducing production accordingly and letting the slump run its course. Once sales had picked up – as they inevitably always did in the next few weeks – production and other budgets could then be remedied as necessary.

Concerning the late payments by the multiple, it was generally agreed that a more pro-active approach was needed – 15 per cent of their trade was carried out with this customer and they could not afford to wait an additional two months for sums of that magnitude. If they did, costly overdraft and loan facilities would soon be needed. That brainstorming session threw up many suggestions, ranging from withdrawing supplies, to offering an improved prompt payment discount structure. After talks, it was decided that Newbabes could not afford to lose the multiple's custom, but at the same time were unable to subsidise it in this way any more. Cathy visited the multiple in person, discussed the dilemma and agreed a new early settlement/bulk buy discount scheme. In effect, the multiple would buy more, pay a little less (proportionately), but more quickly – which suited Newbabes Limited.

Having worked through the pros and cons of each particular course of action raised at the brainstorming session, the team of managers thought further about the likely effects of their chosen responses. If sales improved when and as much as expected, the extra stocks produced could be used as the 'plus 10 per cent' buffer originally planned, capital expenditure would need to be delayed slightly to preserve an on-going, positive cashflow and profits would be down a little – but not too much. If the slump carried on – and the knock-on effects worsened – then some of the more extreme ideas suggested might need to be considered, and fast. Fortunately, sales (as always) did rise when expected and the problem largely resolved itself.

With regard to the early settlement/bulk buy discount scheme, sales receipts from the multiple would fall in value by some 4 per cent. This would not have a noticeable overall impact because the discount applied only to 15 per cent of the total and could be offset by savings – in the distribution budget (as a result of changing ordered quantities and patterns) and minor cuts in expenditure elsewhere. At the same time, Newbabes would receive larger and more frequent payments that much sooner, which benefited cashflow and the smooth running of the business. Cathy considered this to be a good trade-off, and it proved to be as time passed.

Controlling expenditure

Once the potential, knock-on effects of revenue variances have been calculated and hopefully remedied where appropriate, it is time to go on and take an equally close look at expenditure variances, and along the same lines.

Expenditure may be analysed with regard to:

- price variances
- volume variances
- timing variances.

Price variances

Expenditure–price variance may be sub-categorised in two, broad ways – quite simply, purchase prices of goods and services are more than anticipated, and purchase prices of goods and services are less than predicted. Within these sub-categories, you could separate out expenditure even further in terms of start-up, direct, indirect and capital costs, or whatever is deemed appropriate by your business. On the basis that everything else is unchanged – revenue prices, revenue volumes and expenditure volumes more specifically – then increases in direct and other expenditure prices will reduce gross and net profit respectively and probably harm cashflow too as direct expenditure in particular often has to be paid for in advance of revenues. Clearly, the consequences will be the opposite if the prices decrease.

Evidently, falling purchase prices will normally be considered to be favourable by most firms (unless, of course, the quality of goods and services bought falls too). Equally, if the purchase prices of start-up, direct, indirect and capital expenditure rise, then it will almost certainly be seen as a potential problem that needs to be resolved. Solutions might include buying in bulk to gain discounts or purchasing at lower prices elsewhere. Alternatively, and in order to minimise the effects of the variance, consideration may be given to an appropriate, proportional increase in selling prices, attempting to boost sales volumes via marketing activities and/or reducing other expenditure commitments.

Volume variances

Under this heading, you can sub-divide the variance in a similar manner – the number of goods and services bought is greater than estimated, and the number of products and services purchased is less than planned. Again, it is wise to appraise in terms of start-up, direct, indirect and capital expenditure, or as categorised within your business organisation. All things staying the same – revenue prices, revenue volumes and expenditure prices, most notably – then increased purchases of direct and other ex-penditure items will cut gross and net profit in turn, and strain cash resources. Evidently, the situation will be reversed if volumes are reduced – profits will be higher, and more cash will be around.

If the quantities of products and services purchased are less than predicted, it will normally be considered to be a bonus, with more purchases being viewed as a potential long-term problem. Typically, a business concern will try to resolve it by cutting back – putting less chocolate in the chocolate bars, employing fewer people and expecting them to produce more, or whatever. If this is inappropriate or is unsuccessful, then steps will be taken to limit the possible harm done – selling prices may be put up accordingly, sales volumes encouraged to rise through marketing activities and expenditure on other items trimmed, as relevant.

Timing variances

Expenditure–timing variance can be separated out into two sub-headings – expenditure is made earlier than expected and expenditure is paid out later than envisaged. When outgoings are paid does not normally influence the profits (or losses) of a concern, unless prompt-payment discounts are proferred and taken or borrowings are required to fund payments and are then charged for, added to indirect expenditure and thus lower net profit. Clearly though, it will have a huge impact on the company's cashflow, for better or for worse. Paying early reduces cash resources to hand, whilst delaying payments increases the cash circulating within the organisation.

Making payments as late as possible is often seen as being a sensible option – as long as suppliers and other creditors are not offended and do not restrict supplies in the future. At the same time, paying out earlier than is necessary – perhaps before associated or covering revenues are obtained – is viewed as being unwise and potentially dangerous, especially for cash-starved businesses. There are numerous ways of delaying expenditure and generally improving cashflow – minimising stock levels of raw materials, component parts and finished goods for resale, reducing manufacturing times and sales, and taking full advantage of credit terms and suppliers' tolerance.

As with revenue variances, it is advisable to work through the possible consequences of expenditure–price, –volume and –timing variances in relation to your personal circumstances. For example, being able to buy raw materials and component parts at reduced prices appears to be a significant advantage, but may not be in practice if the alternative supplier's delivery is erratic, and production schedules cannot be maintained, thus damaging volumes sold and in turn, profit levels.

Similarly, you do need to contemplate the roll-on effects of any actions you take to eliminate variances. As an example, raising selling prices to compensate for increased direct expenditure may mean a proportion of customers take their business elsewhere, thus leading to a fall in volumes and eventually, profit levels.

Reducing stocks of raw materials and component parts may improve cashflow, but might mean that the firm is unable to satisfy a sudden and unexpected demand for its goods which would have a negative impact on sales volumes and profits. Figure 6.3 is an action checklist which should assist you in controlling expenditure. Case study 6.3 shows how to rectify expenditure variances.

It is sensible to adopt a measured, step-by-step approach to controlling expenditure. Being able to say 'yes' to the following questions indicates that you are tackling expenditure variances in an appropriate manner, and are therefore most likely to succeed.

	Yes	No		Yes	No
Are purchase prices higher or lower than expected?	☐	☐	Profits?	☐	☐
			Cashflow?	☐	☐
Have you identified the effects of this?	☐	☐	Have you decided how to deal with this volume variance?	☐	☐
On budgets?	☐	☐			
On profits?	☐	☐	Do you know what the results of this will be?	☐	☐
On cashflow?	☐	☐	Is expenditure paid for sooner or later than planned?	☐	☐
Do you know how to amend this price variance?	☐	☐	Have you appraised the roll-on effects of this?	☐	☐
Have you worked through the consequences of your actions?	☐	☐	Upon budgets?	☐	☐
			Profits?	☐	☐
			Cashflow?	☐	☐
Are the quantities purchased more or less than anticipated?	☐	☐	Have you spotted a remedy for this timing variance?	☐	☐
Have you estimated the knock-on effects?	☐	☐	Do you realise what the consequences of your actions might be?	☐	☐
Regarding budgets?	☐	☐			

Figure 6.3 Controlling expenditure: an action checklist

CASE STUDY 6.3   **Rectifying expenditure variances**

Towards the end of the 1998–9 trading period, one of the suppliers of raw materials and component parts included in Steve's production budget increased its prices by 12 per cent, some 8 per cent more than expected. The reasons given were the rise in transport costs from overseas combined with adverse, exchange rate fluctuations. As these items made up nearly 60 per cent of the finished product, such a significant price rise could not pass unnoticed and without negative, knock-on effects on Steve's budget, gross, and eventually, net profits. Cashflow suffered slightly too.

At the following management meeting, Steve stood up and outlined the variance and its probable impact. He then suggested various solutions, questioning their advantages, disadvantages and likely consequences. In particular, he talked about staying with the supplier, paying the higher prices and absorbing them within the firm's profits. Alternatively, the higher prices could be offset by reducing other expenditure – and he identified the marketing budget with its (free of charge) display stands, units and materials as an obvious area for investigation. He wondered whether it was wise to pay for and supply stands for their products to retailers who then used them to display other, rival goods!

Another option was to continue buying raw materials and component parts from the same supplier, paying the increased prices and then passing these on to Newbabes' customers by way of similar, proportionate price rises. Obviously, there was a danger here that some customers – and particularly the all-important multiples – might then look elsewhere to those up-and-coming competitors. Finally, Steve indicated that he could seek a replacement supplier who might be able to provide comparable goods at better prices, although he would need to be careful to ensure that quality and service were maintained at acceptable levels.

The management team eventually decided to absorb part of the increase into their profits, with the balance being covered by cuts in the advertising and promotional expenditure in the marketing budget. Reluctantly, they felt they could not put up their selling prices at this time as customers would simply turn to their rivals for goods – although this did remain an option for the future. Likewise, they knew that finding competitively priced *and* reliable alternative suppliers was an almost impossible task at the present moment – but again, it was a possibility for future consideration. This compromise solution was a pragmatic, rather than an ideal, one and it worked well in practice.

Making changes

Hopefully, you will be in a position to initiate personally any actions needed to remedy revenues and/or expenditure variances in your budget – perhaps chasing up sales orders and monies, delaying the purchase of new equipment, or whatever. On occasions, these and other actions carried out by your colleagues will have to be discussed and approved by the whole budget committee, depending upon their likely knock-on effects. Of course, the more significant variances may not be corrected (or not enough) and therefore, changes will need to be made to:

■ your budget

■ other budgets

■ the master budget.

Your budget

Amending your budget will normally take place with the approval of – and after a meeting with – the budget committee. Assuming that the proposed changes are relatively self contained (in that they do not have a roll-over effect on fellow budgets) and minor (in that they do not adversely affect the master budget), then this approval will usually be given automatically. It is sensible to keep monitoring your budget in the same careful and conscientious manner thereafter, studying and checking revenues and expenditure regularly, identifying and attending to variances promptly and drawing the budget committee's attention to problems, as and when appropriate. At some stage – possibly when the first quarter, six month or annual period is ending – it is advisable to review your performance to date. Figure 6.4 is an action checklist concerning this.

Other budgets

Changes to other budgets will probably be given the go-ahead by the budget committee if they too are self-contained and of a relatively minor nature. Those changes – perhaps regarding sales revenues – that will have an impact on related budgets will need to be worked through completely so a full and accurate picture of *all* the likely consequences (and subsequent changes to linked budgets) can be ascertained and accounted for. This process is illustrated in the first half of Case study 6.4.

At some point after your budget has been set, monitored for a while and hopefully adhered to, it is advisable to look back over your budgeting activities to date to learn from your experiences. Typically, you will want to do this after the first three months of your budget have passed, and regularly thereafter. Thinking about these questions may be beneficial:

	Yes	No		Yes	No
Did you begin by finding out all you could about the types of budget in your firm?	☐	☐	Were notes made about the types, amounts and timings of revenues anticipated?	☐	☐
Were the advantages of budgeting considered?	☐	☐	Were additional notes compiled about the types, amounts and timings of expenditure estimated?	☐	☐
Did you think about its disadvantages too?	☐	☐			
Did you discover everything possible about the budgetary procedures in your organisation?	☐	☐	Did you create a basic, attractive and compatible budget forecast form?	☐	☐
Was the 'limiting factor' in your business identified early on?	☐	☐	Was it pencilled in fully and carefully – down the side, across the top and in the middle?	☐	☐
Did you recognise the external influences on your budget and all of the possible effects?	☐	☐	Did you produce a complete, clear and accurate final version?	☐	☐
Did you also spot the internal influences and all of their potential effects?	☐	☐	Were the make-up and activities of the budget committee in your firm known to you in advance?	☐	☐
Was advice sought from a wide range of informed sources?	☐	☐	Did you perform well at the budget committee meeting; both as a speaker and a participant?	☐	☐

Figure 6.4 Reviewing your performance: an action checklist

	Yes	No		Yes	No
Did you find out how your budget affected and was affected by the company's master budget?	☐	☐	Did you also check on the types, amounts and timings of expenditure going out; and often enough?	☐	☐
Were easy-to-administer and regular monitoring procedures established, all starting at the lowest possible levels?	☐	☐	Were significant revenue and expenditure variances and their causes identified?	☐	☐
Did you and your team study the types, amounts and timings of revenues being received; and at frequent intervals?	☐	☐	All in all, did you do well?	☐	☐
			Have you learned from any mistakes?	☐	☐

CASE STUDY 6.4   **Making changes**

Both Mary and Steve had experienced problems with their all-important sales and production budgets – Mary had recorded lower than expected sales at one time, plus delays in payments by a leading multiple retailer, whilst Steve had had difficulties with rising prices for raw materials and component parts. The consequences of these, the actions required to resolve them and the pros and cons of the actions had been identified, and discussed, and the decisions made, to let the slump run its course, to negotiate a new deal with that particular customer and to cut parts of the marketing budget and use the firm's profits to absorb price rises.

The likely results of these discussions then had to be appraised and related budgets amended accordingly. Evidently that lull in sales (and corresponding lull in revenues, however temporary) would affect subsequent production levels and timings of capital expenditure even if sales rose as expected (which they did). Similarly, the revised deal necessitated adjusted sales, distribution and indeed other, individual budgets as compensatory cuts in expenditure had to be made everywhere. As indicated, a proportion of the increased costs of raw materials and component parts was offset by reducing advertising and promotional outgoings from the marketing budget.

Not surprisingly, the effect of these numerous amendments – albeit some short-term and others relatively minor in nature – was to alter the master budget itself. That sales lull had a temporary but significant effect on cashflow and a permanent impact on profits. The new pay deal reached with a major customer had a long-lasting, positive effect on cashflow too. The rising costs of raw materials and component parts meant that gross profit would be down – as would net profit, but *not* as much because of the cuts being made in overhead expenditure. In short, a new cash budget, budgeted profit and loss account and balance sheet had to be drawn up, allowing for these changes.

Fortunately, the overall impact of these various changes was not too adverse and the 1998–9 trading period concluded to Cathy and Steve's satisfaction with the master budget producing good results for Newbabes Limited. This left Cathy, Steve, Raj, Mary and Adam to look towards 1999–2000 with some confidence. The whole budgeting process began again – establishing a sales budget forecast, production budget forecast and so on. Work commenced well in advance …

The master budget

Of course, changes to your and other budgets will mean that the company's cash budget, budgeted profit and loss account and budgeted balance sheet have to be altered, sometimes substantially. It may be that these alterations prove to be unacceptable – cash and profit levels are too low, as examples – and the budgets need to be looked at again in committee and revised, so that they are achievable, *and* the end results are all satisfactory. The second half of Case study 6.4 describes what often happens in practice.

SUMMARY

1 To adhere to a budget as closely as possible, significant variances have to be identified and dealt with so that revenues are achieved and expenditure is controlled, as expected. Occasionally, problems will have to be passed upwards and changes made to this and other budgets.

2 Variances need to be spotted, categorised and their causes calculated. Variances can be categorised in numerous ways:
- revenue–price variance
- revenue–volume variance
- revenue–timing variance
- expenditure–price variance
- expenditure–volume variance
- expenditure–timing variance
- minor variances

3 The effects of revenue variances have to be appraised, and harmful variances rectified, whenever possible. Such variances should be looked at in terms of:
- price
- volume
- timing

4 The impact of expenditure variances has to be assessed too, with damaging variances remedied, so far as possible. Expenditure variances should be viewed with regard to:
- pricem
- volume
- timing

5 Some variances cannot be eliminated and changes must then be made to:
- your budget
- other budgets
- the master budget

Key budgeting questions need to be asked about: forecasting budgets, setting the master budget and managing budgets.

CHAPTER SEVEN

Budgeting: common questions and answers

- Forecasting budgets

- Setting the master budget

- Managing budgets

- Summary

As a non-financial manager trying to gain a broader knowledge and understanding of budgeting within your organisation, you should now have a much better idea of what it involves. However, most managers studying this subject for the first time will still have a number of questions about various aspects of budgeting which they want answered. Key budgeting questions need to be asked about:

- forecasting budgets
- setting the master budget
- managing budgets.

Forecasting budgets

The initial stages of budgeting – discovering what you need to know, preparing and then composing budget forecasts – provide the foundations for later success, when you will hopefully move on to master and maintain budgets in an effective manner.

Here are some of the questions that are asked most often by non-financial managers reviewing these early activities:

- How many budgets should be drawn up by a business?

- How should we decide on the headings and sub-headings for the particular budgets?

- How do we allocate expenditure which is incurred across several departments and sections?

- How far ahead should we budget?

- In what ways can the disadvantages of introducing a budgetary system be minimised?

- What happens if there isn't a limiting factor on our budget?

- Which have the greater impact on budgets: external or internal influences?

- How can we ensure that our revenue figures are accurate?

- How can we guarantee that the expenditure figures are as accurate as possible?

- Which are best to use: standardised company forms or self-produced ones?

How many budgets should be drawn up by a business?

It really depends upon individual circumstances, and in particular the structure, traditions and attitudes of the firm concerned. For example, large and diverse businesses tend to compose many budgets; usually for each department and even section which has responsibility for generating revenues and/or controlling expenditure. Smaller firms may compose just one – their master budget, in effect. Likewise, centralised businesses which seek to restrict decision-making and control processes to key employees only might limit the number of budgets drawn up, whereas those concerns which prefer to delegate to lowest levels could produce more.

There is no right or wrong answer. In essence, it can be argued that however few or many budgets are composed, the same basic process should take place – gathering information, developing estimated revenue and expenditure figures, agreeing them, checking actual revenue and expenditure figures, and so forth. Whether these tasks are carried out informally by staff or more formally by managers working with a budget does not matter as much as the fact that they are done, *and* done regularly and carefully.

How should we decide on the headings and sub-headings for the particular budgets?

Again, there are no hard and fast rules here, and much depends upon personal preferences. For example, in what ways the sales director wants to view sales – by agent, product, region or whatever. Ideally though, headings and sub-headings should be the same, wherever possible, throughout the firm and the budget forecasts. For example, if one departmental or sectional budget has a sub-heading of 'postage/stationery' whereas another has one for 'postage', others for 'pens and pencils', 'paper', 'miscellaneous items' and so on, then putting together a master budget becomes unnecessarily tricky and time consuming. Thought does need to be given as well to how easy it is going to be to collect information under these headings after the budget has been set and is being monitored.

How do we allocate expenditure which is incurred across several departments and sections?

A good example of this would be 'electricity'. In this case, each and every department uses it, especially 'production'. 'Administration' receives and records the bill, and 'finance' pays it, but to which budget (or budgets) is the expenditure allocated? A difficult question, and one which is answered in different ways from business to business. In a small firm, this may be a fairly insignificant point – all employees are told to use electricity wisely, the bill is received, noted in the budget and paid. That, by and large, is that. With larger businesses, who may be concerned that each department and section is, to a certain degree, a viable stand alone unit, the issue may be a more serious one.

In such circumstances, it is commonplace for an estimate to be made of how much electricity is used by the various departments and sections and notional expenditure figures to be allocated to their budgets on the basis of this assessment. Clearly, this approach can be applied to other areas of expenditure – rent, rates, gas and so forth –

in order to judge more accurately how far each department and section is paying its way. In theory, this can be a sensible thing to do, not least because it would otherwise mean that 'admin's' budgeted and actual expenditure would be horrific! However, it is important to be aware that monitoring will have to be completed more carefully with increased levels of cross-referencing and checking taking place. Also, do be conscious that some departments and sections are supportive rather than operational. They may not 'pay their way' in strict financial terms but are essential nonetheless.

How far ahead should we budget?

The majority of firms will budget on a year-to-year basis, with their budgeting period matching their trading year. Typically, a budget will be drawn up some six months before it is due to commence – perhaps September 1999 for the period March 2000–1, for example. Ideally, budgeting will be conducted on an on-going basis with amendments being made as and when necessary. Do not look too far into the future, as forecasting becomes more subjective and unreliable the further ahead you go.

In what ways can the disadvantages of introducing a budgetary system be minimised?

Without doubt, the advantages of budgeting – whereby it acts as a plan, a co-ordinator and so on – do outweigh the disadvantages. Nevertheless, drawbacks do exist and need to be tackled. Major criticisms concern the increased levels of paperwork, and the time taken up in completing this extra documentation. Others are associated with the perceived inflexibility of budgets and employees' resistance to them, often because they are seen as being restrictive and limiting.

> The majority of firms will budget on a year-to-year basis, with their budgeting period matching their trading year. Typically, a budget will be drawn up some six months before it is due to commence.

Rather than dealing with each disadvantage individually, it is better to approach them as a whole, attempting to develop a culture which takes account of all the concerns. Everyone should be involved with budgeting as far as they can – helping to collect information for budget forecasts, being aware of the budgets they are working to and why, and having the opportunity to comment, as and when appropriate. Everything should be kept as simple as possible too

– minor and repetitive checking tasks should be passed down to the lowest level, built into working practices and done informally with regular, formal checks on a limited number of budgets carried out by managers as part of their duties.

What happens if there isn't a limiting factor on our budget?

Almost certainly there will be, even though it may not have been pointed out to you by those higher up the organisational ladder. As often as not, the limiting factor on many departmental and sectional budgets will be an unspoken one of expectation – that they will not exceed last year's (or by not more than a certain percentage), will complement allocated ones and generally fit in. It is advisable to find out well in advance of preparing a budget forecast exactly what limits apply in your situation, and why. It could be argued that this unspoken pressure of being expected to conform to earlier figures – when circumstances may have changed drastically – is an unreasonable one.

Which have the greater impact on budgets: external or internal influences?

Impossible to say, as it depends on the individual situation. The influences which have the greatest impact on budgets – whether of external or internal origin – are those which have not been identified well in advance, taken account of when forecasting and monitored carefully thereafter with adjustments being made to the budget as and when appropriate. Although customers, competitors, suppliers and fellow budgets have the greatest influence on a budget, almost any factor can have a huge impact if unaccounted for beforehand.

> The limiting factor on many departmental and sectional budgets will be an unspoken one of expectation – that they will not exceed last year's (or by not more than a certain percentage), will complement allocated ones and generally fit in.

How can we ensure that our revenue figures are accurate?

It is highly unlikely that estimated revenue figures will prove to be wholly accurate six to 18 months after they have been set – indeed, a variance of more than 10 per cent either way would be considered to be an achievement in most instances. To anticipate revenue figures as well as you can, you need to take fully into consideration any limiting factors, influences from outside of the firm, and within, and then gather together as much information as you are able to about the types, amounts and timings of revenue. The timing of incoming payments is often the hardest to predict.

How can we guarantee that the expenditure figures are as accurate as possible?

Again, it is not easy to estimate expenditure figures months in advance – although it tends not to be quite as difficult as predicting revenues where so much depends on the successes and even whims of customers, the activities of existing and new competitors, and so forth. Once more, limiting factors, external and internal influences must be allowed for, and types, amounts and timings of expenditure then established. Timing is just as important as the amounts paid out, especially for smaller businesses with cash concerns.

Which are best to use: standardised company forms or self-produced ones?

It really does not matter – *as long as* the form is straightforward enough to be completed fully, clearly and accurately, looks attractive and allows information to be taken from it without confusion or difficulty. If standardised company forms are available, then it would be diplomatic to use them, whatever their weaknesses. Hopefully, they will be good enough to be of relevance to all departments and sections drawing up budgets.

Setting the master budget

Once the budget forecasts have been composed, they are usually then submitted to a budget committee for inclusion within a master budget and subsequent authorisation, possibly after some amendments have been made to them to ensure they all fit together properly.

Most non-financial managers will have additional questions that need to be answered about this key stage in the proceedings. Typically:

- How relevant is a budget committee?
- What exactly is a budget manual?
- Will we have to attend a budget committee meeting?
- How important is a budget committee meeting?
- How can we ensure that our budget forecasts will be accepted as they stand?
- Why does one master budget contain four diverse documents?
- How significant is the master budget to the budgeting process?

How relevant is a budget committee?

It varies substantially from one organisation to another. In some, it performs a very dominant role – issuing precise instructions on how budget forecasts should be compiled and when, studying forecasts and compiling a master budget from them, and re-issuing heavily amended budgets which must be adhered to – or else! In other firms, a financial director (or someone of similar standing) will take a supervisory and co-ordinating role with many budgeting decisions being delegated to departmental managers and sectional heads acting together in unison.

In many respects, it could be argued that the greater the degree of control exercised by a budget committee (or whoever is in charge), the easier it is for inexperienced, non-financial managers to produce and maintain acceptable budgets. With guidelines to be followed closely, the committee having to be convinced about the validity of a particular budget and answered to if or when actual results deviate from estimated ones, there may be less room for errors, or possibly even carelessness, to enter into the process. Of course, as you gain in experience, such a system may be restricting and frustrating, but it is not disadvantageous at this stage.

What exactly is a budget manual?

To all intents and purposes, a budget manual is simply a written set of instructions telling all departmental managers and section heads responsible for composing and managing budgets exactly how to do it. Clearly, it is essential, for example, that all budget forecasts are drawn up in a standardised format using the same headings, sub-headings and so forth (as far as possible) so that they can be interpreted easily and information taken from them promptly for the master budget. These instructions must be followed to the letter.

Will we have to attend a budget committee meeting?

Possibly, but it does again depend largely on the business concerned. In some instances, you may have your budget forecast approved, rejected or amended by your line manager or the financial director (or similar) responsible for budgeting. Just as likely, you might be expected to attend a meeting along with every other section head and departmental manager in the company, to discuss and perhaps negotiate your individual budget forecasts. More extensive and vigorous questioning tends to take place at a committee meeting, with plenty of 'what if?' questions being asked. This can be beneficial, helping to confirm the strengths of the forecast, or highlight any shortcomings. It can be embarrassing, but is worthwhile nonetheless.

How important is a budget committee meeting?

If you have to attend one, then it's important! In many respects, it can be a turning point in the budgeting process – a time when estimated revenue and expenditure figures are put to the test, budget forecasts are provisionally drafted together in discussion to see how they combine in terms of profits and cash flow, and negotiations take place for some payments to be delayed, others brought forward and so on. It is essential that you have prepared well and are able to participate fully in the talks so that you have a better chance of having your budget forecast approved, or at least as much of it as possible.

How can we ensure that our budget forecasts will be accepted as they stand?

You cannot guarantee that your budget forecast will be approved completely by the committee – not least because there will be many forecasts which have to fit together well, showing acceptable levels of profit and cash resources on an on-going basis. The chances of them all coming together successfully are remote – so some adjustments will have to be made somewhere. However, you can certainly improve the prospects of widespread acceptance by showing you have taken account of any limiting factors and have thought fully about external and internal influences before compiling your forecast, *and* can back up the types, amounts and timings of revenues and expenditure stated with good reasons, and independent evidence whenever possible.

Why does one master budget contain four diverse documents?

Simply because the term 'master budget' is an all purpose one which is defined (slightly) differently from one company to another. Ideally, it should contain four documents – the existence of a profit budget, cash budget, a profit and loss account and a balance sheet are what are needed to give the firm a sufficiently broad *and* detailed understanding of its whole financial position. Some (mainly smaller) businesses refer to their profit budget as their 'master budget' and fail to compose a cash budget and/or projected annual accounts – a serious shortcoming as this presents an incomplete financial picture of the way ahead. Perhaps this is one reason why they experience so many cash difficulties.

> You can certainly improve the prospects of widespread acceptance by showing you have taken account of any limiting factors and have thought fully about external and internal influences before compiling your forecast.

How significant is the master budget to the budgeting process?

It is crucially important, and in three ways. First, it concludes the planning stage, pulling in and merging together the numerous budget forecasts in an effective manner. Second, it shows whether or not the business and its forthcoming activities will be liable in terms of profits, cash flow, assets and liabilities. Third, it begins the control stage, providing the entire business with a financial framework to work within and towards.

Managing budgets

The later stages of budgeting – keeping track of and adhering to budgets – are perhaps the most worrying for non-financial managers, especially those who are new to the function.

Most of what can go wrong occurs now – even though these problems and difficulties may have been caused by inaccurate forecasting, weeks or maybe months ago! Numerous questions are raised about this time, including:

- How often should a budget be monitored?
- When should we be notified of variances between estimated and actual figures?

- What are the most common types of variance to look for when monitoring revenues?

- What are the main causes of revenue variances?

- What are the likely effects of revenue variances?

- How can revenue variances be resolved?

- What are the main types of variance to watch out for when monitoring expenditure?

- What causes expenditure variances to occur?

- How might expenditure variances affect a budget?

- What can be done about expenditure variances?

- Isn't changing a budget a sign of failure?

How often should a budget be monitored?

Informally, all of the time – staff should be permanently noting and checking actual and estimated revenues and expenditure as a matter of routine, and be trained to report anything out of the ordinary to you as and when it arises. More formally, a budget has to be monitored by you 'as required' which may mean every day, or once a week or month. It depends mainly on how volatile and unpredictable the situation is. For example, if cash flow is perilous and incomings are paid erratically, then the position may need to be checked daily. If expenditure is occasional and largely as predicted then less frequent monitoring is required. Monthly checks are advisable in most cases though just to keep abreast of the situation, however steady it may seem to be.

When should we be notified of variances between estimated and actual figures?

As soon as any significant variance becomes apparent to a member of your staff – and only you (and they) can decide exactly what is classified as 'significant'. Plus or minus 10 per cent of what was expected and/or anything which has a noticeable knock-on effect on this budget or others is often viewed as a trigger point. One off and minor, reversible variances may then be handled by you, with more serious ones being dealt with by consultation, perhaps with the budget committee.

What are the most common types of variance to look for when monitoring revenues?

There are three in particular. 'Price' – where the price paid for your goods and services is less (or occasionally more) than expected. 'Volume', when the number of products and services sold is lower (or perhaps higher) than anticipated. 'Timing' – where the prices received and volumes sold are as predicted, but monies are received later (or possibly earlier) than budgeted for. It is sensible to be aware not only of these variances – which, after all, are relatively easy to identify – but also of their causes, effects and the probable solutions to them. You also need to recognise that the variances often arise simultaneously rather than separately. This can sometimes confuse the situation, making them hard to distinguish individually, and deal with.

What are the main causes of revenue variances?

Incompetence, most likely – although few managers will admit to it. Quite simply, an inaccurate forecast was made – limiting factors, external and internal influences were not taken fully into consideration, over-optimistic figures were included with regard to amounts and timings of revenue, and so on. More often, managers will refer to selling prices going up or down to match rivals' prices, more or less being sold because of increased competition, and payments coming in earlier or later due to customers' financial difficulties. Fine, but how much responsibility should be accepted by the manager who drafted the budget? Some, surely.

What are the likely effects of revenue variances?

In theory, revenue variances mean that figures are better *or* worse than expected and the consequences are therefore either favourable *or* unfavourable – theoretically, it is 50–50 either way. In practice however, 90 per cent of revenue variances are negative, with revenues being lower or later than anticipated. Many would say that this is a direct result of managers being too bullish in the first place. The likely effects of negative revenue variances are clear – reduced gross profit and net profit and potentially, cash shortages. These need to be addressed, and quickly, if the budget is to get back on course.

How can revenue variances be resolved?

As the major reason for variances is management misjudgement, then one way of resolving them is to redraft figures in the light of greater knowledge and expertise. Clearly, it is wiser to face up to this and accept 'less' and 'delayed' revenues in future, rather than trying to adhere to an unrealistic budget which differs noticeably from what is actually happening. If attempts are made to boost profits and cash flow – perhaps because a genuinely unpredictable factor affected the budget – then thought needs to be given to the consequences of any actions. For example, if selling prices are put up, quantities sold may fall. Likewise, prompt payment discounts may improve cash flow, but not profits; and which is more important to the firm?

What are the main types of variance to watch out for when monitoring expenditure?

Three types of variance are of some concern. 'Price variance' exists when you have had to pay more (or perhaps less) for products and services for use within the business. 'Volume variance' means that the quantities purchased are greater (or sometimes lower) than was anticipated. 'Timing variance' occurs when payments are made sooner or later than was estimated in the budget. The causes, effects and possible remedies to these variances should be understood as fully as possible. It is also important to realise that the different types of variance often occur at the same time, and need to be identified and tackled singly.

What causes expenditure variances to occur?

By far the most common reason for expenditure variances arising within a budget is that whoever set the budget in the first place underestimated (or less likely overestimated) the types, amounts and timings of expenditure to be incurred during the period in question. Unfortunately, few will admit that it is as simple as that! Usually, the explanations given will deflect the blame – for example, suppliers' price rises were greater than anticipated, or staffing costs have increased excessively. All valid points perhaps, but maybe the manager who estimated these figures originally should have been more realistic at that time.

How might expenditure variances affect a budget?

Strictly speaking, expenditure variances may be either in the firm's favour or not – although the bulk of them do tend to have a negative impact with more money having to be paid out than was expected, and perhaps sooner. If expenditure is greater than anticipated then gross and/or net profits will be lower. Should money be paid earlier than predicted then profits will remain unaffected in most cases, although cash flow will be harmed, perhaps to a significant degree.

What can be done about expenditure variances?

Whenever any variances occur, it is a good idea to ask whether they are a consequence of a management miscalculation or a sudden, wholly unexpected change in external and/or internal factors. If the actual expenditure could have been predicted more accurately through closer initial investigations and better assessments, then it is wise to alter the budget accordingly so that you deal with what is really happening rather than what you wanted to happen. Alternatively, if the situation is reversible, attention must be given to possible solutions – finding a cheaper supplier, making internal economies, paying later or whatever. It is advisable also to contemplate the ramifications of solutions. They may resolve this problem: but will they create others?

Isn't changing a budget a sign of failure?

No, not at all. Ideally, each and every budget should be flexible, with regular checks being made on it, actual and estimated performances compared, limiting factors, external and internal influences re-evaluated, and amendments being implemented as and when appropriate. A budget must not be a rigid, unyielding document with everything being categorised as black or white, right or wrong, success or failure. It should be seen as a loose framework, constantly evolving to take account of changing situations with figures being moved about, replaced and even put back in again as you gain a broader and deeper understanding of your circumstances. The only 'failure' would be to set an unrealistic budget and then try to stick to it, come what may. Budgeting needs to be approached in a pragmatic manner.

SUMMARY

1 Most non-financial managers will have various questions about forecasting budgets, including these:

- How many budgets should be drawn up by a business?

- How should we decide on the headings and sub-headings for the particular budgets?

- How do we allocate expenditure which is incurred across several departments and sections?

- How far ahead should we budget?

- In what ways can the disadvantages of introducing a budgetary system be minimised?

- What happens if there isn't a limiting factor on our budget?

- Which have the greater impact on budgets: external or internal influences?

- How can we ensure that our revenue figures are accurate?

- How can we guarantee that the expenditure figures are as accurate as possible?

- Which are best to use: standardised company forms or self produced ones?

- How important are budget forecast forms?

2 It is important to possess a full knowledge and understanding of setting the master budget. These are some of the key questions about this stage of the budgeting process:

- How relevant is a budget committee?

- What exactly is a budget manual?

- Will we have to attend a budget committee meeting?

- How important is a budget committee meeting?

- How can we ensure that our budget forecasts will be accepted as they stand?

- Why does one master budget contain four diverse documents?

- How significant is the master budget to the budgeting process?

3 The majority of non-financial managers will seek answers to the following questions about managing budgets:

- How often should a budget be monitored?
- When should we be notified of variances between estimated and actual figures?
- What are the most common types of variance to look for when monitoring revenues?
- What are the main causes of revenue variances?
- What are the likely effects of revenue variances?
- How can revenue variances be resolved?
- What are the main types of variance to watch out for when monitoring expenditure?
- What causes expenditure variances to occur?
- How might expenditure variances affect a budget?
- What can be done about expenditure variances?
- Isn't changing a budget a sign of failure?

Three potential problem areas are now worthy of further attention: the profit budget, the cash budget and projected annual accounts.

Budgeting:
typical problems
and solutions

- The profit budget

- The cash budget

- Projecting annual accounts

- Summary

_____

In order to complete the knowledge and understanding needed to have a firm grasp of budgeting, it is a good idea to take a broader perspective of the process, looking at some of the most common problems that may be faced on a company-wide basis, and to consider various possible solutions to them. Three potential problem areas are now worthy of further attention:

- the profit budget
- the cash budget
- projected annual accounts.

The profit budget

A profit budget is the document which specifies the anticipated sales, direct costs, indirect costs and profits or losses of a business over a particular period of time. More often than not, it will span the organisation's accounting year and be split into 12 monthly sections. An example of the first six months of a profit budget is set out in Figure 8.1. It can be seen that this is a working document and problems have arisen with regard to the amounts of revenue and expenditure being received and paid out. These need to be thought about in relation to:

- causes
- effects
- potential solutions.

Causes

The two key problems highlighted in the profit budget are relatively common ones. 'Sales' are noticeably lower than anticipated and the 'cost of materials' is significantly higher. Potentially, these are very serious, if not even fatal, difficulties, especially when combined together to squeeze profits from both sides. You may also be able to recognise other variances in the budget and can perhaps address these yourself once the two leading problems have been dealt with.

To begin with, it is advisable to identify all of the possible causes of these difficulties to decide subsequently which ones are valid here. Falling sales revenue can have many causes – not least reduced output and/or selling prices, adverse publicity, increased competition and falling demand. Higher costs of materials may be as a result of more goods being used within the production process, raised prices, having to find a new, less competitively priced supplier and so on. Perhaps you can think of more.

Effects

If the revenues being received fall and/or the amounts of expenditure being paid out rise then the knock-on effects are relatively easy to identify, and usually very quickly. Gross profit will be that much lower (and consequently so too will net profit) in the first instance. With regard to the second, net profit will be reduced, perhaps substantially.

The combined effect of these two negative factors will exacerbate the problem, possibly even placing the firm in a loss making position. In some cases, a cash rich business can keep trading indefinitely, although ultimately it will be forced to address this underlying weakness, and maybe even cease trading.

Potential solutions

The solution to any difficulty of this nature should be to study and then tackle its underlying cause(s). In this example, immediate and obvious remedies might include raising selling prices and/or initiating a publicity campaign to deal with falling revenues and locating more competitively priced suppliers in relation to rising expenditure. Nevertheless, it is also sensible to contemplate the roll on effects of such responses – increased prices may mean demand dropping further, and new suppliers may be good on price but poor in other respects such as product quality or delivery times. For the example given, insufficient research had been conducted – the figures being roughly what would have been expected if more detailed discussions had taken place with customers and suppliers. Assumptions had been made on the basis of opinions rather than facts.

> The two key problems highlighted in the profit budget are relatively common ones. 'Sales' are noticeably lower than anticipated and the 'cost of materials' is significantly higher. Potentially, these are very serious, if not even fatal, difficulties, especially when combined together to squeeze profits from both sides.

The cash budget

A cash budget – or cash flow forecast as it is also known – is the document which illustrates how cash will come into and go out of a business over a specified period of time. Normally, it will cover the forthcoming year, and be subdivided into 12 monthly periods, although some firms prefer 13, four weekly periods which may be better suited to their financial and accounting systems and procedures.

Figure 8.2 is an example of a cash budget. The first six months of it are shown. Evidently, the 'estimated' columns have all been completed. The first three months' 'actual' and 'variance' columns have been filled in too. At this stage, it has become apparent that there are some problems which need to be dealt with, and promptly.

PROFIT BUDGET	Month: 1/99			Month: 2/99			Month: 3/99		
	Est.	Act.	Var.	Est.	Act.	Var.	Est.	Act.	Var.
Sales (A)	30,000	29,500	(500)	30,000	29,500	(5,000)	30,000	28,000	(2,000)
Less:									
Direct costs									
Cost of materials	10,000	10,000	0	10,000	10,000	0	10,000	11,000	(1,000)
Wages	12,000	12,000	0	12,000	12,000	0	12,000	12,000	0
Gross profit (B)	8,000	7,500	(500)	8,000	7,500	(500)	8,000	5,000	(3,000)
Gross profit margin (B ÷ A x 100%)	26.66	25.42	—	26.66	25.42	—	26.66	17.86	—
Overheads:									
Salaries	4,000	4,000	0	4,000	4,000	0	4,000	4,000	0
Rent, rates, water	2,000	2,000	0	2,000	2,000	0	2,000	2,000	0
Insurance	200	250	(50)	200	250	(50)	200	250	(50)
Repairs, renewals	200	200	0	200	200	0	200	200	0
Heat, light, power	100	100	0	100	100	0	100	100	0
Postage	50	50	0	50	50	0	50	50	0
Printing, stationery	100	120	(20)	100	120	(20)	100	120	(20)
Transport	200	200	0	200	200	0	200	200	0
Telephone	100	100	0	100	100	0	100	100	0
Professional fees	100	100	0	100	100	0	100	100	0
Interest charges	—	—	—	—	—	—	—	—	—
Other	—	—	—	—	—	—	—	—	—
Total overheads (C)	7,050	7,120	(70)	7,050	7,120	(70)	7,050	7,120	(70)
Trading profit (B–C)	950	380	(570)	950	380	(570)	950	(2,120)	(3,070)
Less depreciation	400	400	—	400	400	—	400	400	—
Net profit	550	(20)	—	550	(20)	—	550	(2,520)	—

Figure 8.1   Profit budget

Month: 4/99			Month: 5/99			Month: 6/99			TOTALS		
Est.	Act.	Var.	Est.	Act.	Var.	Est.	Act.	Var.	Est.	Act.	Var.
60,000			60,000			60,000			270,000		
20,000			20,000			20,000			90,000		
24,000			24,000			24,000			108,000		
16,000			16,000			16,000			72,000		
26.66			26.66			26.66			26.66		
4,000			4,000			4,000			24,000		
2,000			2,000			2,000			12,000		
200			200			200			1,200		
200			200			200			1,200		
100			100			100			600		
50			50			50			300		
100			100			100			600		
200			200			200			1,200		
100			100			100			600		
100			100			100			600		
—			—			—			—		
—			—			—			—		
7,050			7,050			7,050			42,300		
8,950			8,950			8,950			29,700		
400			400			400			2,400		
8,550			8,550			8,550			27,300		

169

Fortunately, these difficulties relate purely to the timings of revenue and expenditure rather than surpluses or shortfalls in their types and amounts. It is sensible to consider them in terms of their:

- causes

- effects

- possible solutions.

Causes

Looking at the half completed cash budget, it can be seen that there are two potential major problems. 'Cash from debtors' is being delayed somewhat and 'payments to suppliers' have gone out earlier than planned – both fairly typical, commonplace difficulties experienced by the vast majority of businesses at one time or another. There are various, other minor variances too, and you may wish to address the causes, effects of, and possible solutions to these, yourself after the two main problems have been worked through.

So why is 'cash from debtors' – in this instance, customers with credit facilities – being received later than expected? A non-financial manager facing this needs to jot down probable causes in turn and then study them individually in order to ascertain their validity in the situation. Misjudgement is the obvious reason – bills were always going to be paid at that time but the manager didn't realise this in advance. Perhaps customers' finances have worsened suddenly, in which case they need to be contacted to ensure that sales do not continue to be made to those who cannot pay for them on time, or at all. You may be able to list other possibilities as well.

The causes of earlier 'payments to suppliers' – typically of raw materials and component parts – have to be investigated too, and then evaluated. There are a whole host of reasons for this – miscalculation on the part of the manager, changed accounting procedures within the firm, a new discount structure introduced by suppliers, a more aggressive credit control policy being adopted by suppliers being amongst the most likely ones. Perhaps you can think of other ones, that might be appropriate in your position.

Effects

Whenever any revenues are received later than estimated and/or expenditure is paid earlier than anticipated, then the effects are always the same – the cash situation worsens possibly to the point where there are insufficient funds to keep trading. Obviously, this is increasingly likely when the two adverse influences are combined as they are in this example. Often, the significance of the timings of revenues and expenditure are not taken fully into consideration, with greater emphasis being given towards the amounts involved – *until* the cash runs out and it is too late to remedy the situation.

Possible solutions

The obvious solution to late revenues and early expenditure is simply to reverse the process – chasing up debts more vigorously so that revenues are paid earlier and holding on to expenditure until later when there are sufficient cash resources available to make payments, *and* retain enough in reserve for other outgoings. Sometimes, this will be an appropriate approach. Debtors can be encouraged to pay up sooner by employing various tactics including a revamped discount policy, prompter billing arrangements and more regular contact, reminders and even threats when necessary. Incoming bills can be kept in the system for an extra 30 days or whatever before being paid, to slow expenditure.

However, such an approach can backfire – offering discounts may cut into profits, prompter billing might mean employing more staff, threats can lead to trade being taken elsewhere and delaying payments might lead to further supplies being withheld, possibly permanently. Thus, it is important to study carefully the causes of problems and to choose a remedy which matches them as closely as you can. In this instance, 'cash from debtors' figures were just too optimistic and the budget needs to be redrafted with 60 days being allowed for rather than 30 (although 30 days remains a target to work towards) 'Payments to suppliers' were being processed almost immediately by an over-enthusiastic new member of staff, who needed to be told to hold on to payments for at least 30 days if not slightly longer in some cases.

> The obvious solution to late revenues and early expenditure is simply to reverse the process – chasing up debts more vigorously so that revenues are paid earlier and holding on to expenditure until later when there are sufficient cash resources available to make payments, *and* retain enough in reserve for other outgoings.

CASH BUDGET	Month: 1/99			Month: 2/99			Month: 3/99		
Receipts:	*Est.*	*Act.*	*Var.*	*Est.*	*Act.*	*Var.*	*Est.*	*Act.*	*Var.*
Cash sales	25,000	26,000	1,000	25,000	25,000	0	25,000	26,000	1,000
Cash from debtors	20,000	19,000	(1,000)	25,000	23,000	(2,000)	25,000	18,000	(7,000)
Capital introduced	–	–	–	–	–	–	–	–	–
Total receipts (A)	45,000	45,000	0	50,000	48,000	(2,000)	50,000	44,000	(6,000)
Payments:									
Payments to suppliers	25,000	26,000	(1,000)	25,000	27,000	(2,000)	23,000	27,000	(4,000)
Salaries, wages	8,500	8,500	0	8,500	8,500	0	8,500	8,500	0
Rent, rates, water	–	–	–	12,500	12,500	0	–	–	–
Insurance	2,500	2,900	(400)	–	–	–	–	–	–
Repairs, renewals	–	–	–	–	–	–	500	700	(200)
Heat, light, power	–	–	–	500	600	(100)	–	–	–
Postage	100	80	20	100	90	10	100	110	(10)
Printing, stationery	1,000	1,000	0	–	–	–	–	–	–
Transport	400	450	(50)	400	400	0	500	550	(50)
Telephone	500	450	50	–	–	–	–	–	–
Professional fees	–	–	–	–	–	–	–	–	–
Capital payments	500	500	0	500	500	0	500	500	0
Interest charges	100	100	0	100	100	0	100	100	0
Other	100	100	0	100	100	0	100	100	0
VAT payable	–	–	–	3,500	3,300	200	–	–	–
Total payments (B)	38,700	40,080	(1,380)	51,200	53,090	(1,890)	33,300	37,560	(4,260)
Net cashflow (A–B)	6,300	4,920	(1,380)	(1,200)	(5,090)	(3,890)	6,700	6,440	(10,260)
Opening bank balance	1,500	1,500	–	7,800	6,420	–	6,600	1,330	–
Closing bank balance	7,800	6,420	–	6,600	1,330	–	23,300	7,700	–

Figure 8.2   Cash budget

Month: 4/99			Month: 5/99			Month: 6/99			TOTALS		
Est.	Act.	Var.	Est.	Act.	Var.	Est.	Act.	Var.	Est.	Act.	Var.
20,000			20,000			30,000			145,000		
25,000			20,000			20,000			135,000		
—			—			—			—		
45,000			40,000			50,000			280,000		
26,000			26,000			23,000			148,000		
8,500			8,500			8,500			51,000		
—			12,500			—			25,000		
—			—			—			2,500		
—			—			500			1,000		
—			500			—			1,000		
100			100			100			600		
—			—			—			1,000		
500			500			500			2,800		
500			—			—			1,000		
—			—			2,000			2,000		
500			500			15,000			17,500		
100			100			100			600		
100			100			100			600		
—			4,000			—			7,500		
36,300			52,800			49,800			262,100		
8,700			(12,800)			200			17,900		
23,300	7,770		32,000			19,200			1,500		
32,000			19,200			19,400			19,400		

Projected annual accounts

Completed profit and cash budgets enable a budgeted profit and loss account and a budgeted balance sheet to be drawn up – in short, projected annual accounts. A profit and loss account is the financial statement which states the anticipated sales, total costs and profits or losses of a firm over a given period of time, normally one year. An example is shown as Figure 8.3.

A balance sheet is the (accompanying) financial statement indicating the concern's assets and liabilities at that time and showing how its activities were financed during the preceding period. Figure 8.4 is an example of one. Both examples are taken from a small, owner-operated business run from home. They are especially straightforward so that subsequent explanations are not obscured by detailed financial data and calculations.

One of the main problems of producing annual accounts is that it can be difficult to interpret these properly just by looking at them – and this is especially true if you are a non-financial manager with an untrained eye. Sales look good, gross and net profits seem acceptable, current assets are greater than current liabilities and everything adds up – but there is always that nagging doubt that all is not as well as it appears to be.

If you are shown a projected profit and loss account and a balance sheet during the budgeting process, you will without doubt have various questions which you want answered. As examples – Are we buying and selling efficiently? How does our gross profit compare with the average in our trade or industry? Are we spending too much or too little on overheads? Is the business financially secure? And so forth. It is unlikely that you can resolve these issues simply by perusing the accounts in front of you.

The solution is to apply financial ratios to the figures that you have, which will then allow you to reach more informed conclusions about how well the business is or will be doing if everything unfolds as predicted.

There are many ratios which can be employed in this situation and some of the most useful ones are shown in Figure 8.5 (see page 177) for ready reference purposes, and are as follows:

- gross profit margin
- net profit margin
- expenditure ratios
- current ratio

	£	£
		58,000
Sales:		
Opening stock	20,000	
Purchases	25,000	
Closing stock	15,000	
Cost of sales		30,000
Gross profit		28,000
Overheads:		
Rent, rates, water	8,000	
Wages	3,000	
Transport	1,300	
Heat, light, power	1,200	
Printing, stationery	1,000	
Telephone	800	
Depreciation	600	
Professional fees	600	
Postage	500	
Insurance	400	
Repairs, renewals	200	
Miscellaneous	100	
Total		17,700
Net profit		10,300

Figure 8.3   A profit and loss account

- acid test ratio

- stock turnover ratio

- debtor days ratio

- creditor days ratio

- sales per employee ratio

- profit per employee ratio

- investment efficiency ratio.

The following examples are taken from the accounts reproduced in Figures 8.3 and 8.4.

	£	£
Fixed assets:		
Equipment	1,000	
Vehicle	800	
		1,800
Current assets:		
Stock	15,000	
Debtors	4,000	
Cash	500	
	19,500	
Current liabilities:		
Creditors	4,500	
Bank overdraft	3,000	
	7,500	
Net current assets		12,000
Net assets		13,800
Financed by:		
Capital	12,000	
Profit	10,300	
Drawings	(8,500)	
		13,800

Figure 8.4   A balance sheet

Gross profit margin	=	$\dfrac{\text{Gross profit} \times 100}{\text{Sales}}$
Net profit margin	=	$\dfrac{\text{Net profit} \times 100}{\text{Sales}}$
Expenditure ratios	=	$\dfrac{\text{Expenditure} \times 100}{\text{Sales}}$
Current ratio	=	$\dfrac{\text{Current assets}}{\text{Current liabilities}}$
Acid test ratio	=	$\dfrac{\text{Debtors} + \text{Cash}}{\text{Current liabilities}}$
Stock turnover ratio	=	$\dfrac{\text{Cost of sales}}{\text{Average stock}}$
Debtor days ratio	=	$\dfrac{\text{Debtors} \times 365}{\text{Sales}}$
Creditor days ratio	=	$\dfrac{\text{Creditors} \times 365}{\text{Purchases}}$
Sales per employee ratio	=	$\dfrac{\text{Sales}}{\text{Number of employees}}$
Profit per employee ratio	=	$\dfrac{\text{Profit}}{\text{Number of employees}}$
Investment efficiency ratio	=	$\dfrac{\text{Sales}}{\text{Fixed assets}}$

Figure 8.5   Accounting ratios

Gross profit margin

This ratio enables you to examine the relationship between sales and direct costs and shows how successfully the firm is buying, selling and trading – all of which are likely to determine if it is going to succeed (or fail) on a long term basis.

The ratio is given below and is followed by an example relating to the accounts just shown. The resulting figure can be compared alongside the trade average which is a useful yardstick for measuring the firm's performance.

$$\frac{\text{Gross profit} \times 100}{\text{Sales}}$$

$$\frac{£28,000 \times 100}{£58,000} = 48.28 \text{ per cent}$$

Net profit margin

Net profit margin expresses net profit as a percentage of sales – and is important because it indicates whether the business is truly profitable after all of the costs have been met. If it is not – or is perhaps not doing as well as in previous years or as hoped – then attention needs to be turned upon expenditure, and to reducing parts of it in some way.

$$\frac{\text{Net profit} \times 100}{\text{Sales}}$$

$$\frac{£10,300 \times 100}{£58,000} = 17.76 \text{ per cent}$$

Expenditure ratios

It can be helpful to take each area of expenditure – whether 'administration', 'finance', 'distribution', 'rent, rates, water', 'wages' or whatever – to view them as percentages of sales. This is especially useful for comparing year-on-year changes and identifying causes of any reduction in the net profit margin.

The examples reproduced below after the ratio are for 'rent, rates, water' and 'heat, light, power'.

$$\frac{\text{Expenditure} \times 100}{\text{Sales}}$$

$$\frac{£8,000 \times 100}{£58,000} \quad = \quad 13.79 \text{ per cent}$$

$$\frac{£1,200 \times 100}{£58,000} \quad = \quad 2.07 \text{ per cent}$$

Current ratio

The current ratio is a simple one, which shows if the business is solvent or not.

If all the short term debts to the bank, suppliers and the like had to be paid up tomorrow, there must be (at least) sufficient funds to meet them and, hopefully, enough would be left over to keep trading. If not, thought must be given to increasing assets and reducing liabilities somehow.

$$\frac{\text{Current assets}}{\text{Current liabilities}}$$

$$\frac{£19,500}{£7,500} \quad = \quad £2.60 \text{ (of assets for every £1.00 of liabilities)}$$

Acid test ratio

Of course, if a firm had to settle all of its current liabilities immediately, it would be difficult to convert stocks into cash very quickly so it may be wiser to exclude these from the calculation.

The resulting, acid test ratio, when applied to the relevant figures from the accounts, may reveal that the financial position is not quite as secure as it first appeared, and steps may need to be taken to remedy this.

An obvious suggestion would be to reduce stock levels as promptly as possible, with the 'extra' cash being retained in case of need.

$$\frac{\text{Debtors} \times \text{Cash}}{\text{Current liabilities}}$$

$$\frac{£4,500}{£7,500} \quad = \quad £0.60 \text{ (of assets for every £1.00 of liabilities)}$$

Stock turnover ratio

As a general rule, for most trades and industries, stock should be kept as low as possible and turned over quickly, thus freeing cash resources and making the most efficient use of funds.

Clearly, the rate of turnover will vary according to circumstances but can be compared with the trade or industry average for assessment purposes:

$$\frac{\text{Cost of sales}}{\text{Average stock}}$$

$$\left(\text{Average stock} \quad = \quad \frac{\text{Opening stock} + \text{Closing stock}}{2} \right)$$

$$\frac{£30,000}{£17,500} \quad = \quad 1.71 \text{ times per annum}$$

$$\left(\frac{£20,000 + £15,000}{2} \quad = \quad £17,500 \right)$$

Debtor days ratio

This ratio highlights the number of days taken by customers to settle their bills.

Not surprisingly, debts to the firm need to be paid as promptly as possible in order that a satisfactory cash flow is maintained at all times – and should certainly be received before equivalent monies are paid over to creditors. The time taken can be appraised alongside previous years' figures and what is considered to be acceptable in the marketplace.

$$\frac{\text{Debtors} \times 36}{\text{Sales}}$$

$$\frac{£4,000 \times 365}{£58,000} = 25 \text{ days to be paid}$$

Creditor days ratio

This accompanying ratio indicates how long it takes for the business to meet its debts. Careful attention needs to be given to the figure produced by this ratio – in theory, it should be longer than that of the debtor days ratio and, in terms of cash flow, as late as possible. However, thought must also be directed towards the benefits of paying earlier for prompt payments discounts, and to sustaining a decent working relationship with suppliers.

There is little point in paying very late if you'll never be able to obtain raw materials from that source again!

$$\frac{\text{Creditors} \times 365}{\text{Purchases}}$$

$$\frac{£4,500 \times 365}{£25,000} = 66 \text{ days to pay}$$

Sales per employee ratio

Sales per employee measures the income produced by each member of the firm's workforce. It enables you to monitor progress from one year to the next, and to make comparisons with other, similar businesses operating in the same trade or industry.

The profit and loss account and balance sheet reproduced as Figures 8.3 and 8.4 are from a firm which is run by an owner-manager with one employee – perhaps not the best of examples, but adequate for explanatory purposes.

$$\frac{\text{Sales}}{\text{Number of employees}}$$

$$\frac{£58,000}{2} \quad = \quad £28,000$$

Profit per employee ratio

Alternatively, judgements can be made with regard to the net profit generated on average by each employee of the concern.

Again, it allows performances to be set alongside those of earlier years or in other, comparable businesses active in the same marketplace.

$$\frac{\text{Profit}}{\text{Number of employees}}$$

$$\frac{£10,300}{2} \quad = \quad £5,150$$

Investment efficiency ratio

Investment efficiency indicates how efficiently the firm is using its fixed assets in terms of the sales produced by each £1 of equipment, machinery and so on. In essence, it shows whether or not fixed assets are earning their keep:

$$\frac{\text{Sales}}{\text{Fixed assets}}$$

$$\frac{£58,000}{£1,800} \quad = \quad £32.22 \text{ per } £1.00$$

SUMMARY

1 Two typical problems that occur most often within a profit budget involve falling revenues and rising expenditure. It is important to be aware of their:

- causes
- effects
- potential solutions

2 There are two major areas of concern with regard to a cash budget – revenues being received later than anticipated and expenditure being made earlier. It is advisable to understand their particular:

- causes
- effects
- possible solutions

3 It is difficult to interpret a profit and loss account and a balance sheet without some assistance. The following ratios can be helpful:

- gross profit margin
- net profit margin
- expenditure ratios
- current ratio
- acid test ratio
- stock turnover ratio
- debtor days ratio
- creditor days ratio
- sales per employee ratio
- profit per employee ratio
- investment efficiency ratio

To conclude, look back over what has been covered so far to ensure that you have taken account of everything you need to know about.

The non-financial manager's budgeting checklist

By this stage, you should possess all of the information needed to have a sound understanding of budgeting, and what it involves. To conclude, you ought to look back over what has been covered so far to ensure that you have taken account of everything you need to know about.

It is sensible to approach this review on a chapter-by-chapter basis, as follows.

What you need to know about budgeting

- Are you aware of the different types of budget that exist, and are within your particular firm?
- Do you recall the advantages of introducing a budgeting system?
- Are you conscious of the possible disadvantages?
- Have you thought about how these could be minimised, or even eliminated altogether?
- Do you know of the typical budgeting procedures that take place, and what happens in your organisation?

How to prepare budget forecasts

- Was all of the background information needed to compile a budget forecast gathered together carefully and fully?

- Limiting factors identified, and allowed for?

- External influences recognised, and taken into consideration?

- Internal influences noted, and accounted for?

- Appropriate sources of advice referred to, and listened to as well?

- Were forthcoming revenues then anticipated cautiously?

- In terms of types?

- With regard to amounts?

- Were timings contemplated carefully as well?

- Was upcoming expenditure then estimated thoroughly?

- The particular types?

- The specific amounts?

- Were the timings thought about too?

How to compose budget forecasts

- Did you use one of the firm's budget forecast forms, or create your own?

- Was it simple and straightforward to use – both by you *and* any colleagues who wanted to refer to it?

- Was it attractive, helping to convey the right image of your forecast?

- Was it also compatible with other forms being submitted?

- Did you accumulate the contents in an effective manner?

- Were appropriate headings and sub-headings put down the side?

- Were the right periods and sub-periods placed across the top?

- Were realistic figures put into the middle?

- Did you produce an acceptable final version?

- Was it fully complete?

- Were all your figures clear and easy to understand?
- Were they all scrupulously accurate as well?

What you need to know about submitting budget forecasts

- Are you aware of the role of a budget committee, both generally and in your specific business?
- Do you know who sits on this committee, with special regard to your own firm?
- Do you recall the main activities of a budget committee, and what it does within your particular organisation?
- Have you participated successfully in a committee meeting?
- Did you prepare fully?
- In what ways?
- Did you handle the meeting itself in an efficient manner?
- What exactly did you do?
- Did you follow up the meeting?
- How did you do this?
- Are you aware of what a master budget consists of?
- Can you read a profit budget?
- How about a profit and loss account?
- Can you study a cash budget effectively?
- How about a balance sheet?

How to keep track of budgets

- Have appropriate monitoring procedures been established?
- Are they easy to administer?
- Are they carried out regularly?
- Are they completed at the lowest possible levels?
- Do you study revenues carefully when filling in the budget?

- Paying particular attention to the types of revenue received?
- Taking account of the amounts too?
- With special regard to the timings as well?
- Do you check expenditure conscientiously when completing the budget?
- In relation to the types of expenditure incurred?
- Concerning the amounts of expenditure going out?
- With particular regard to the timing of payments?

How to adhere to budgets

- Are you able to identify different types of variance?
- So what is revenue–price variance?
- Revenue–volume variance?
- How about revenue–timing variance?
- What is expenditure–price variance?
- Expenditure–volume variance?
- How about expenditure–timing variance?
- Do you know how to achieve revenues?
- Can you resolve price variances?
- Deal successfully with volume variances?
- Tackle timing variances effectively?
- Do you know how to control expenditure?
- Can you reduce price variances?
- Eliminate volume variances, or at least as far as possible?
- Rectify timing variances, and promptly too?
- Are you ready to make changes, as and when variances cannot be resolved satisfactorily?

Budgeting: common questions and answers

- Did you have any questions about forecasting budgets?
- What were they?
- Have they been answered satisfactorily?
- Did you have any additional queries about setting the master budget?
- What were these queries?
- Have they been answered?
- Was there anything else you wanted to know about managing budgets?
- What questions did you have?
- Have they been dealt with effectively?

Budgeting: typical problems and solutions

- Are you able to spot problems in a profit budget?
- Do you know how to tackle them?
- Can you identify difficulties within a cash budget?
- Do you know how to deal with them?
- Can you interpret a profit and loss account by using financial ratios?
- What ratios should you use?
- Can you interpret a balance sheet as well?
- What ratios are most relevant with regard to this financial statement?
- Do you now know all you need to know about budgeting and what it involves?

Glossary

Accounting ratios: Calculations which enable accounts to be quantified precisely and a firm's financial status and performance to be identified with a greater degree of accuracy.

Administration budget: Statement of estimated administrative expenditure over a particular period; one of the easiest to produce.

Balance sheet: Statement showing a firm's assets and liabilities at the end of a given period of time, and how its activities have been funded.

Budget: Estimate of revenue and/or expenditure to be generated and/or incurred over a forthcoming period of time. A framework to work within and towards.

Budget assumptions: Set of company-wide assumptions which everyone has to allow for and abide by when setting budgets.

Budget committee: Group of people responsible for approving forecasts, composing the master budget and issuing other budgets.

Budget guidelines: Instructions for compiling, submitting and monitoring budgets. Usually issued by the budget committee.

Budget holders: Those people responsible for overseeing major functional and departmental budgets.

Budget manual: File or booklet incorporating budget assumptions, guidelines and other miscellaneous facts and figures.

Budget officer: Person responsible for co-ordinating the budgetary system and procedures.

Budget period: Length of time covered by the budget. Often one year, and coinciding with the calendar or firm's accounting year.

Capital: Finance to be injected into a firm, either by its owners or financiers, such as banks or building societies.

Capital assets: Permanent items of long term use to a business such as land, premises and equipment.

Capital expenditure: Outgoings or non-consumable items of long term, permanent use to a firm – plant, equipment and machinery, as examples.

Capital expenditure budget: Statement of estimated expenditure on capital items over a specified period of time, normally 12 months. Often a straightforward enough budget to compile, and easy to overlook during monitoring procedures.

Capital goods: Items of long term value to a business; including land, buildings, equipment and machinery.

Cash budget: Statement of a firm's cash inflows and outflows over a specific period of time.

Cash flow: Term used to describe the process of monies coming into and going out of a business as it trades.

Composite budget: Statement created from an amalgamation of other budgets – sales, production, marketing and the like. Many smaller businesses refer to this as the 'master budget'.

Current assets: Ever changing items which come and go as a business conducts its activities; typically stock and cash.

Current liabilities: Short term debts which need to be settled in the near future, usually 12 months. Examples include bank overdrafts and taxes due.

Debtors: Individuals or organisations which owe money to a firm – usually late paying customers.

Departmental budget: Statement of estimated revenue and expenditure of a department over a set period of time, typically one year.

Depreciation: Amount by which a capital asset reduces in value over a given period of time; normally calculated on an annual basis.

Direct expenditure: Outgoings which vary directly with production and/or sales levels; raw materials and component parts, as examples.

Direct labour: That part of the workforce which is directly involved with producing and/or selling goods and services.

Direct materials: Those materials which are used up during production and/or sales procedures; component parts, for example.

Distribution budget: Statement of estimated expenditure on transport, deliveries and associated activities over a particular period; typically 12 months.

Expenditure: Total outgoings, often viewed in terms of 'capital', 'direct', 'indirect' and 'start-up' expenditure.

Fixed assets: Items of long term use to a business; typically premises, equipment and machinery. Also known as 'capital assets'.

Fixed costs: Outgoings incurred which are not directly related to production and/or sales levels. Examples include rent and rates. Also known as 'indirect expenditure' and 'overheads'.

Forecast: Prediction of revenue and/or expenditure to be generated and/or incurred over a forthcoming period of time. In many respects, a proposal to be discussed and studied in due course.

Gross profit: The profit remaining after direct expenditure has been deducted from sales.

Gross profit margin: Figure highlighting the relationship between sales and profit. Expressed as a percentage, calculated by dividing gross profit by sales and multiplying by 100.

Indirect expenditure: Costs incurred by a firm, often on a regular basis, which are not linked directly to levels of production and/or sales. Rent is an obvious example. Also known as 'fixed costs' and 'overheads'.

Indirect labour: The part of the workforce which is not involved directly in producing and/or selling goods, and is therefore employed largely in an administrative and supportive capacity.

Indirect materials: Those materials which are purchased but not used up in production and/or selling procedures.

Limiting factor: Key, overriding influence which has a significant constraining effect on a firm's financial activities, and budgets in particular.

Liquid assets: Items of short term value to a business; used during trading activities. Cash is an example. Better known as 'current assets'.

Management by exception: Management style adopted whereby only important and/or exceptional matters are drawn to a manager's attention by employees.

Master budget: Term used to describe a set of accumulated and co-ordinated, key documents – a cash budget, a profit budget, a profit and loss account and a balance sheet.

Net assets: The sum of net current assets and fixed assets, as featured in a firm's balance sheet.

Net current assets: Figure calculated by deducting current liabilities from current assets, where assets are greater than liabilities. Also known as 'working capital'.

Net current liabilities: Figure reached by subtracting current liabilities from current assets, where liabilities exceed assets.

Net liabilities: The sum of net current liabilities and fixed assets where the former is greater than the latter.

Net profit: Sum remaining after direct and indirect expenditure have been deducted from sales. Not to be confused with 'gross profit'.

Operational budgets: Those budgets which are composed for sections and departments whose work is linked to the value of business being achieved. 'Marketing' is an example.

Overheads: On-going costs of a firm, paid out regardless of production and/or sales levels. Also known as 'fixed costs' and 'indirect expenditure'.

Production budget: Document specifying the quantities of goods to be produced during a period of time, along with the costs of production.

Profit and loss account: Statement showing a firm's sales and costs at the end of a given period of time, and any profits or losses outstanding.

Profit budget: Document illustrating how a firm's sales and costs were generated and incurred on an on-going basis over a specified period of time.

Revenue: Total incomings from all sources, but primarily sales in most instances.

Sales budget: Document detailing the expected sales to be received over a given period of time, typically one year.

Sales income: Revenues received from the sale of goods and services. Usually viewed by product group, territory or marketplace.

Start up expenditure: Costs incurred as a consequence of doing, producing or selling something for the first time.

Support budgets: Those budgets compiled for sections and departments which act in a supporting capacity, eg 'Administration'.

Variable costs: Outgoings which vary directly in line with production and/or sales levels. Also known as 'direct costs' or 'direct expenditure'.

Variances: Differences between estimated and actual revenue and expenditure.

Variation report: Document recording estimated and actual revenue and expenditure figures, plus their variances.

'What if?' questions: Hypothetical questions raised to assess the accuracy and reliability of forecasted revenue and expenditure figures.

Working capital: Sum remaining after current liabilities have been deducted from current assets. Also known as 'net current assets'.

Index